T0330585

SUSTAINABLE DEVELOPMENT

Papers from the 6th EADI General Conference,
Oslo, 27–30 June 1990

Sustainable Development

edited by
OLAV STOKKE

FRANK CASS · LONDON
in association with
The European Association of Development Research
and Training Institutes (EADI) Geneva

First published 1991 in Great Britain by
FRANK CASS AND COMPANY LIMITED
Gainsborough House, 11 Gainsborough Road,
London E11 1RS, England

and in the United States of America by
FRANK CASS
c/o International Specialized Book Services, Inc.,
5602 N.E. Hassalo Street, Portland, Oregon 97213

British Library Cataloguing in Publication Data

Sustainable development.
I. Stokke, Olav II. The European journal of
development research. ISSN 0957–8811
330.91724

ISBN 0-7146-3449-2

Library of Congress Cataloging-in-Publication Data

Sustainable development / edited by Olav Stokke.
    p. cm.
    ISBN 0-7146-3449-2
    1. Economic development--Environmental aspects. 2. Environmental
policy. I. Stokke, Olav, 1934–
HD75.6.S86 1991
363.7'058--dc20
                                                91-32068
                                                CIP

This group of studies first appeared in a Special Issue on Sustainable Development of
The European Journal of Development Research, Vol. 3, No. 1
published by Frank Cass & Co Ltd

Contents

Foreword

Olav Stokke

The European Association of Development Research and Training Institutes (EADI) organised its 6th General Conference in Oslo, 27–30 June 1990. The general theme was 'New Challenges for European Development Research', with particular reference to the changes taking place in Europe, East and West, and to sustainable development. More than 200 papers were presented – in the plenary sessions, in two parallel, special sessions on the two main themes, and in the sessions of 23 working groups and five *ad hoc* panels. It is from this harvest that the editors of the previous and the present issues of the EJDR have selected contributions. No.2 (1990) focused on the changes in Europe and their effects. The present issue focuses on the other main theme of the conference, sustainable development.

The concern with ecological development is a surprisingly recent phenomenon, although most of the issues involved are familiar in the development debate. In the early 1970s, the publication of *Limits to Growth* (Meadows *et al.*, 1972) attracted widespread attention and the United Nations Conference on the Human Environment in Stockholm in 1972 (with an alternative conference bringing together NGO environmental activists – the salt and pepper in the environmental drive) brought the issue squarely on to the agenda of international politics for the first time. Since then, this concern has been increasingly institutionalised at national and international levels, nationally through the establishment of ministries (and ministers) of the environment, internationally most markedly through the establishment of the United Nations Environment Programme (UNEP) in Nairobi in 1972. However, it was not until the publication of the report of the World Commission on Environment and Development (WCED), *Our Common Future* (1987), that the issue emerged as a priority theme on the international agenda, and there is now to be a World Conference on Development and the Environment in Rio de Janeiro in 1992.

The Chairman of the WCED, Ms Gro Harlem Brundtland, was invited, as a keynote speaker, to take stock of the follow-up of the recommendations of the WCED after three years and to draw up the perspectives and challenges ahead. She outlines the state of our global environment, including the alarming trend of deforestation, the loss of species and biological diversity, and desertification. World poverty, uneven development and population growth are identified as the roots of the problem.

Sustainable development must become an integral part of the economic reconstruction of Europe; some of the enormous scientific and technological resources used for military purposes must in the new situation be transferred to environment and development, she argues. With reference to the damage to the environment in Central and Eastern Europe, she feels confident that the European nations together will be able to reverse the negative trends, although the costs involved will be staggering. 'We have the financial resources. We have the scientific knowledge and a capability for technological innovation . . . We are witnessing new political will . . .'

The threat to the atmosphere is presented as the potentially most serious global issue, involving climatic change, with powerful economic, social and political consequences. Although encouraged by recent positive signals, the road leading to an effective climate convention will have to deal with difficult issues, including the use of energy, which today is not regulated by any kind of international agreement. Listing the challenges ahead, she concludes that the real test case will come in the developing countries, where the most rapid growth in energy consumption is now occurring. All our capacity for innovation needs to be mobilised to meet the challenge to combine the necessary Third World development with environmental concerns. 'What we need is a general mobilisation of our collective resources, both in the public and private sectors, to achieve a shift of direction of the world economy into tracks that would make it truly sustainable.' Institutional reform, both at regional and global levels, is deemed necessary to improve the efficiency of decision-making, to get stronger international institutions, even with supranational authority for decision-making and monitoring and to ensure compliance on issues which are vital for sustainable development.

Harold Brookfield, in his contribution, concentrates on 'environmental sustainability', with special focus on the land-based-resources aspect of the problem. Reviewing the literature on the theme, he observes that, even down to the mid-1980s, most development theorists remained blind to the extensive literature that, since the 1950s, has warned us of the evils of erosion, desertification, resource degradation, pollution and the destruction of amenity that Third World development has created; the notion that 'growth' is ultimately unsustainable is traced back to J.S. Mill's *Principles of Political Economy* (1848).

In his search for a clarification of the sustainability concept, reviewing the different approaches of the 1980s, Brookfield starts from the recognition that, while there is indeed a set of natural limitations, there may also be a sustainable way out. He finds a strictly conservationist position impracticable for a variety of reasons; change is seen as a natural condition and change at the hands of human beings as inevitable. The role of human activity in relation to nature is to modify ecosystems and to accelerate change in natural systems, while at the same time opening systems further by introducing new elements and shifting others from one place to another. 'Reliance on natural regenerative processes is more than an ideal; it is also technically much the cheapest way of obtaining sustainability.' He sees an insufficiently explored midway path between what he terms the rigid, natural determinism of the 'limits to growth' and the steady-state schools, on the one hand, and 'technological cornucopianism', on the other. The mediating force is successful human adaptive artifice.

It is through such processes that sustainable development has been achieved in the past. The difference in our time is primarily a quantitative one. The impact on resources and the environment has accelerated exponentially through population growth, major increases in per capita consumption, and the global quest for rapid development. Brookfield concludes that sustainable development (1) involves 'maximizing and optimally distributing the net benefits of economic development, so far as these can be achieved, while establishing and reaffirming the conditions of security under which the services and qualities of natural resources can be maintained, restored or improved into the foreseeable future'. To make development sustainable, (2) 'it is necessary that natural reproduction of capabilities be not drawn down, that investment in conserving or improving capabilities be undertaken and sustained, so that the environment of future generations becomes a productive and wholesome artefact built of human artifice allied to and enhancing natural reproduction'. However, as environments change in space and time, (3) 'the definition and practice of "sustainable development" must be undertaken in this context of environmental uncertainty'. However, sustainable development needs a strong, civil society, it demands enlightened social intervention and thrust in an interventionist state.

Sukhatmoy Chakravarty, in analysing the implications of ecological sustainability for paradigms of economic growth, with particular reference to the prevailing situation in the Third World, concludes that a free market regime cannot by itself cope with all the issues involved, but that economies relying on central planning and public ownership of land and means of production have also failed in their natural-resource management. Similarities in outcome may have arisen from ignoring certain fundamental, irreversible processes which require a different way of conceptualising the development process. The lot of the majority has not improved and neither new technology nor investment in material capital has enabled them to substitute for the loss of their environmental capital stock, which has been seriously eroded.

Development strategies will have to cope with the poverty problem; the poorer countries must be enabled to grow at rates which produce perceptible changes in living standards. This transition may be speeded up by technological changes in areas of energy transition. Resources released by the reduced production of arms should be used to augment productive capacity, where this is urgently needed. Traditional strategies which take effective note of distributional considerations, intranationally and internationally, need to be devised.

Appropriate policies are necessary to prevent further ecological damage, not just in terms of market forces versus public intervention, but more in terms of institutional changes. Common property resources were traditionally maintained by community participation at the local level; with the advent of development planning and the market, the local involvement has broken down, with negative effects for the environment. Institutional reforms must be supported by economic incentives and disincentives. Public policies must be addressed to the needs of the local populations.

A thorough change in currently held attitudes is seen as an prerequisite to sustainable development. Modern technological developments have changed objective circumstances all round. The *laissez-faire* system can no longer work, because of the growth of interdependence in production, consumption and communications between nations. Multilateral coordination of economic and social policies has become an imperative necessity for the efficient and equitable management of the lives of the planet's inhabitants, according to Sukhatmoy Chakravarty.

The introductory contribution, by Olav Stokke, outlines the setting of the sustainability debate. As international co-operation is considered imperative by all the contributors to this volume, in order to achieve and maintain a sustainable development, the prospects are discussed against the background of the structural changes of the international environment. This discussion is organised around five dimensions: the end of the cold war, the declining role of the state *vis-à-vis* the market, the trend towards increased globalisation, the parallel trend towards increased regionalisation, and the development crisis in the South.

The last two contributions included transcend the level of general analysis by their focus on strategies and means of obtaining effects in line with the general objectives set by the WCED within two areas of great importance, namely Third World commodity exports and climate.

In the first of these contributions, Henk L.M. Kox departs from the Brundtland Commission's emphasis on the need for more effective instruments to integrate environment and development concerns into international trading patterns. The study explores how to integrate the costs of the environmental preservation and exploitation of natural resources in regular international price systems.

In the foreseeable future, commodity production will remain an important export sector for most developing countries, although many of them have tried to shift their activities to a point further down in the production chain. During the 1980s, Third World countries have been compelled to compensate for low prices by producing and exporting larger volumes of commodities, in order to finance their import needs and to service their debts. The IMF and the World Bank have actively pushed in this direction, too, although a vicious circle is involved.

The harmful ecological effects of the production of primary commodities have increasingly become a matter of international concern. Although it is difficult to valuate these costs in monetary terms – as ecological effects have no natural unit of measurement, have no market value and can hardly be forecasted – estimates arrived at by the methods available, in particular the alternative cost method, make it likely that they are substantial and that the hidden environmental subsidy transferred to OECD countries is far from trivial. This would justify an integration of environmental externalities into international commodity prices both for ecological and for economic reasons.

The adjustments necessary for sustainable development could be brought about by regulating output or input, supplemented by monitoring and policing institutions. This would, according to Kox, introduce certain aspects of a command economy. Within a market economy, policies for sustainable development must be concerned about internalising environmental externalities. Commodities produced by ecologically more sound technologies must obtain either a price premium or a cost advantage. Although some progress has been made in developing policy instruments within some OECD countries – and within the EC – based on the principle that 'the polluter pays', it is not considered feasible in an international context, owing to different levels of international development and different priorities. International treaties based on the principle that 'the non-polluter gets paid' seem more promising. International treaties regulating trade in primary commodities might relate to an established tradition in which links are established between the production, consumption and trade conditions of specific primary commodities.

Producers who adapt to alternative, ecological methods of production should be given an *environmental premium* which should be included in the commodity's world market price on a commodity-by-commodity basis. International arrangements and market regulations, therefore, form a prerequisite for the internalisation of this premium. The lessons learned from the UNCTAD-generated Integrated Programme on Commodities of the mid 1970s, with the dual objective of redistribution and price stabilisation, led Kox to the conclusion that stabilisation of *export earnings* was better served by international compensation arrangements of the Stabex type. Environmental protection elements should, Kox argues, be integrated in international commodity agreements – renamed International Environment and Commodity Agreements (IECAs) – and the environmental premium should be fixed on a commodity-by-commodity basis. He outlines the main elements of a research phase and a negotiation phase of such an endeavour. The negotiation process should draw on the long-term self-interests of nations; however, this process would not be free from conflicts between long-term and short-term interests and regional or country-group egoism – and the inclination, on the part of some countries, to become free riders. Kox finds an import toll more appropriate than an export tax as a means of collecting the environmental premium.

The IECA model addresses the *current* costs of environmental protection and reconstruction; the problem posed by the depletion of non-renewable resources has been left out. This also applies to the negative ecological externalities caused by market failures and wrong government policies, which influence the production of primary commodities for export, too; these have to be addressed by other means.

The contribution by Jan van Ettinger, T. Hans Jansen and Catrinus J. Jepma on climate, environment and development serves the primary function of providing background information on the present theme. However, it transcends that aspiration by clarifying policy options and offers a range of policy recommendations involving both priorities and action. The authors discuss measures to mitigate the impacts of climatic change, as well as measures to reduce net omissions of greenhouse gases, asserting that, without a well-designed, internationally co-ordinated plan of action involving the developing countries, there will be no hope of solving the problem of global climatic change. This would need a massive North–South transfer as a major component.

The authors review the interactions between climatic change and development, giving special attention to the potentially adverse effects of ocean warming, sea-level rise and increasing climate variability on development. Measures to mitigate these impacts are outlined and discussed, with particular focus on agriculture, forestry and fishery, on improving infrastructure, and on accelerating socio-economic development, concluding that the highest priority should be given to 'buying time', in order to clear up the remaining uncertainties. In discussing measures to reduce emission levels, primary attention is given to areas where also other environmental and/or economic benefits can be obtained, namely energy use, deforestation and phasing out of chlorofluorocarbons (CFCs). The conclusion here is that although investments dealing with CFCs and reforestations appear to be the most cost-effective policy for the short and long term respectively, a mix of policies should be carefully selected. Energy savings deserve first priority in preventing emissions, and a fuel switch to natural gas provides a means of buying time in the medium term, while alternative energy sources constitute the long-term sustainable option. Finally, a scenario for a minimum and a maximum CO_2 reduction is established and discussed.

OLAV STOKKE
Norwegian Institute of International Affairs

Sustainable Development:
A Multi-Faceted Challenge

Olav Stokke

I. THE SETTING

The main achievement of the World Commission on Environment and Development [*WCED, 1987*] was not so much that it revealed new insights, rather that it placed environmental problems and issues, environmental *concerns*, on the agenda – on the local, national, regional and international levels – more forcefully than ever. The Commission has succeeded in keeping them there, too. The global conference in Brazil next year represents a future landmark in a process which originated from the report.

The future course of this process cannot be foreseen today, although the general aims have gained wide support at the level of declaratory politics from an increasing number of important actors (though with some defensive resistance from some go-slowers) in national and international political arenas. In actual fact, however, these arenas are full of conflicts at all levels – the local, the national and the international – with conflict dimensions between systems at different levels as well. Interests and values conflict, and the time dimension involved complicates the picture even more. However, there are also a few potentials for agreement, particularly the concern for survival in the long term.

A Need for Further Conceptual Exploration

The core concept – *sustainable development* – needs further clarification. This is, in the first place, a task for politicians, but the various disciplines may also provide valuable contributions. As 'sustainability' applies to development within many different systems with different environmental determinants, the concept will almost of necessity be diffuse, even elusive, like other concepts at a similar level of generalisation which have the dual objective of constituting the basis for intellectual discourse (demanding clarity) and guiding the work of a wide variety of political institutions.

The definition offered by the WCED, 'development that meets the needs of the present without compromising the ability of future generations to meet their own needs' [*1987: 43*], may indicate the general direction but little more; it invites further elaboration. The general direction is underscored by reference to its framework: the concepts of 'needs', in particular the essential needs of the world's poor, to which overriding priority should be given, and of the limitations imposed by the state of technology and social organisation on the environment's ability to meet present and future needs. To be operative in terms of the planning and forming of our common future, the definition has to be sharper. Development goals (and then strategies, guidelines and means to attain these goals) within different environments and fields need to be derived from the general definition; today, such a process is only in its initial stage. The various disciplines, with their different approaches and perspectives, may give emphasis to different aspects of sustainability; what matters, however, is the multi-faceted picture emerging from the perspectives of several disciplines and involving not only the natural and social sciences, which so far have been in the forefront, but also the humanistic sciences.

Traditional Economic Growth vs. Sustainable Development

The ecological systems at various levels, ultimately the biosphere, are affected by interests which relate to man's activities over a broad spectrum, locally and globally. The main conflict is between *development in terms of growth*, related to man's utilisation of the available natural resources, renewable and non-renewable, in order to improve the lot of societies and individuals, and the *realisation of an ecologically sound development*. Most major political systems have had economic growth as the primary aim and have pursued development strategies adapted to this aim. This applies certainly to the industrial North (both West and East), particularly during the twentieth century, with devastating ecological consequences (those recently revealed in the East being even more bleak than pessimistic anticipations); and most governments in the Third World have economic growth as their primary aspiration. Over time, the realisation of this goal will, almost of necessity, affect the resources of a finite world.

The Uncertainties Involved

It follows that a major theoretical conflict dimension is *between the present and future generations*, namely how the satisfaction of present needs, as conceived by the present generation, will affect the possibility for future generations to satisfy their needs. The assessments of the various aspects of this conflict involve both matter and norms and are necessarily embedded in ambiguities, even fallacies. Thus, in the same generation, *needs* are conceived differently from one environment and culture to another; how future generations will conceive of their needs may well be beyond our imagination, although calculations may be based on some fixed standards involving what at present are conceived of as basic human needs. Changes in *technologies* may affect the future use of natural resources, too; what human inventiveness may lead to in the future cannot be known today. Changes in *political systems*, in development goals and development strategies, may also influence the utilisation of the environment, for the better but also for the worse, causing yet another uncertainty. Also *norms* relating to the rights of man and the obligations of contemporaries towards future generations may change and cannot be predicted.

A key concept in the sustainability debate is the *carrying capacity* of an ecological system, relating to the taxation of the renewable natural resources. Sustainable growth presupposes, basically, that harvesting will be within the limits of the regenerative capacity of these resources. However, even here uncertainty is manifest. The carrying capacity changes, too; as already indicated, it is affected by technological inventions, for the better or for the worse. It is affected by the way it is used, too. Changes at one level (for instance, in the biosphere) may cause changes at lower levels; environmental changes (for instance, in the rainfall) may affect the carrying capacity of a resource in a local or regional context from one year to the next. More fundamental, *qualitative* changes in the carrying capacity, caused by man or nature (or man and nature in combination), however, may easily escape attention, because they become observable only within relatively long time spans (the desertification of arable land may illustrate the point).

Such uncertainties remind us of the limitations in our present knowledge. They may easily influence the urgency with which environmental problems are dealt with today; the most probable effect will be to relieve the pressures that are being built up against man-made environmental degradation. Confronted with serious threats to the environment, therefore, it would make sense 'to find out that we have been roughly right in due time [rather] than to be precisely right too late' [*NAVF, 1990*].

The Need for Effective Ecological Regimes

However, conflicts relating to the utilisation of resources, with negative environmental effects, are legion also in the present generation, between interest groups at local and national levels within states and between states. Resources are not equally distributed, which causes strains along several dimensions. Both norms and interests are in conflict, at local level, at national level and globally.

At the *local* level, the conflict between the interest of the community and that of its individual members is illustrated in the now classical example given by Hardin [*1968*]. Where the confines are wider, involving many communities, each community may act in a similar way; as surveillance and control will be more difficult to handle and predictably less effective, the fragile common interest will be even more vulnerable *vis-à-vis* selfish interests. In Hardin's example, the commons will, almost of necessity, turn out to be the losers. He may, however, have underestimated the ability of a society, when threatened, to resist assaults on the commons – and may even have misinterpreted the basic perceptions and inclinations of individual members of such societies [*Helland, 1990*]. However, the outcomes of such conflicts affect the ecological systems in which they take place; ecologically negative outcomes, on local and national levels, will be cumulative and in the end affect the planet Earth and its biosphere negatively. Control and enforcement functions are less developed and weaker on the international level than on most local and national levels; this applies to the administration of an ecologically sound development, and to the ability to curb violations of the commons, as well.

The logic involved leads to a need for more, not less, regulation regarding the utilisation of natural resources, involving institutions, laws and enforcement capability locally, at the national level and internationally. And these must emerge from a shared understanding of the ecological imperative. In retrospect, demands of a similar kind, involving effective, international regimes capable of enforcing the decisions arrived at, have been raised on several occasions, in relation to many issues of vital importance to mankind, particularly within a collective security framework. The demand emerging from the environmental imperative, however, easily outbids any of the previous 'utopian' demands. Although concern for the survival of mankind has been the *raison d'être* for these previous 'utopian' demands, they have been more limited in scope: the demands emerging from the ecological imperative are all-embracing.

The challenges confronting our generation – and generations to come – are therefore multi-faceted, involving all the levels, from the local to the global, of many systems – political, economic and cultural – more or less linked to each other and governed by different kinds of 'law'. Different aspirations are in conflict. Developments and decisions at one level of a system affect the developments at others; at the same time, an ecologically viable development cannot be achieved without concerted action at all levels.

In the present global system, almost all decisions that affect the environment (and most other issues) are vested in the political authorities of nation states, both in a formal and in a real sense. However, many decisions, even decisions involving vital issues, tend to evade the norms set by political authorities, nationally or locally, being 'regulated' by the market and the 'laws' and decision-makers governing these arenas, locally, nationally and internationally.

The most glaring vacuum today is to be found at the international level. Although international 'regimes' exist and several of them may influence national decisions, these regimes are today unable to effectively enforce decisions, with a few exceptions (such as the UN Security Council within its limits). Most environmental issues have a global dimension, including those which have attracted most attention in the current debate, centred around the *greenhouse effect* resulting from carbon dioxide being dumped (without effective regulation or control) in the biosphere, with effects for mankind which cannot yet be surveyed. International regimes, agreements and cooperation across the frontiers of nation states constitute fundamental preconditions for handling several issues deemed to be of vital environmental importance. An international regime capable of reaching and enforcing decisions to be applied globally is essential for the management of our common future.

However, formal governmental structures, on local, national and international levels, are not alone in exercising political power – as has been demonstrated in eastern Europe during the last two years by 'grassroots' and non-governmental movements, emerging more or less spontaneously and directed towards political reform, in a situation in which the hegemonic government in the region decided, for a variety of reasons (mostly self-interest but also on the basis of newly stated norms), to loosen its grip on its satellite nations.

The world today is in radical transition along several dimensions. To what extent are the present international systems capable of meeting the 'new' challenge from the environmental imperative? To what extent does the emerging world order give hope for a more sustainable development in the future?

The uneven distribution of benefits and the sharply contrasted conditions of life existing between North and South (without even taking into account the variations within North and South) constitute an overriding conflict dimension at the global level. In an ecological perspective, this conflict gives rise to the more fundamental question of the kind of development to be pursued – involving North and South alike. The most crucial issues in the current debate, involving conflicting norms and interests, may be considered in this perspective.

II. WHAT KIND OF GLOBAL SYSTEM IS EVOLVING?

Since the Second World War, power relationships in the world have, on the surface, been quite stable. However, change only occasionally results from dramatic events; usually it is an ongoing process, albeit recognised and fixed at a certain point in time due to more spectacular events. In the bipolar world system that emerged in the wake of the war, the South played only a marginal part; military, economic and political power was vested in the North and shared by the 'Socialist' North-East and the 'Capitalist' North-West, with the USSR and the US as the hegemonic powers in the two camps.[1] Starting in the late 1950s, the world system gradually became less bipolar. New centres of power emerged both in the 'East' and the 'West'. China de-linked itself from the hegemony of the USSR and, in the West, Japan and the Federal Republic of Germany (FRG), the two losers in the Second World War, gradually emerged as major economic powers, though both maintained a low political profile *vis-à-vis* the hegemonic power.

By the mid-1960s, the 'winds of change' had turned most of the remaining colonial dependencies into independent international actors. Although efforts were made from the very beginning to create unity and an independent position *vis-à-vis* the two blocs, these governments did not succeed in speaking with one voice and several of them were more or less closely aligned with one of the two dominant systems (most of them with the North-West) economically and to some extent also politically, a few even militarily. Their strong voting power in the universal international bodies exaggerated their real power position; it did, however, bring the development issue into the centre of international politics.

These processes have been carried further today – during recent years at an explosive pace. The Socialist North-East has disintegrated almost totally. While its hegemonic power is still a military superpower, it has been exposed as a giant with feet of clay in economic and also in political terms; its ideological foundation has lost its attraction too, not least at home. The hegemonic power in the North-West has also experienced a relative decline in economic and political terms, while retaining its military power basis. Here, the major trend has been towards regionalisation, illustrated by the recently established North American (Canada, USA and soon Mexico) free-trade area and the economic (and political) integration in western Europe. The European Community (EC) will complete an internal market next year and is giving a lead to broader regional co-operation including the present EFTA countries and even the countries of central and eastern Europe. Japan has emerged as the dominant power in the 'South-East' in a setting that may also be characterised as emerging regional co-operation. The rest of the 'South', including countries with quite different power potentials in economic, political and military terms (even countries of a size comparable with entire regions, like China and India), remains disintegrated.

The real power is, therefore, increasingly located in the 'North-West', with the 'South-East' as the main challenger. Decisions governing trade, capital flows and technology are controlled by the governments of the major powers in the North-West (and Japan), by international institutions in which they have the final say and by transnational corporations which have their home bases in these countries. The policies pursued by these governments will therefore be decisive for the kind of world which is left to future generations.

However, what happens in the South will also fundamentally influence our common future; three quarters of the world's total population live in the Third World which accounts for more than two thirds of the earth's land-surface area. The effects of environmental damage do not stop at national frontiers nor are they limited to the region of origin, as illustrated by the thinning of the ozone layer, the greenhouse effect, pollution of the seas and air, and nuclear pollution. This damage results primarily from patterns of 'growth' and consumption in the North. Although the time perspective may be somewhat longer, deforestation and desertification in the South will result in similar damage with global effects.

No wonder, therefore, that the WCED established a strong link between poverty and environmental development, arguing that sustainable ecological development will be dependent upon an effective resolution of problems that are causing poverty globally and at the local level. That conclusion was based both on norms (related to equity and basic human rights) and on observations of the causes involved. However, the complexities, even contradictions, involved in this linkage are easily recognised, whatever the type of growth, but particularly if the patterns of the North are to be copied.[2] The kind of development aimed at – the objectives, strategies, and development patterns – becomes of crucial importance.

What potential – positive and negative – has the evolving international world system for an improved sustainable development in the future? And how will it affect the South? The discussion of these questions will be organised around five dimensions of the changed international environment: the end of the cold war, the declining role of the state vis-à-vis the market, the trend towards increased globalisation, the parallel trend towards increased regionalisation, and the development crisis in the South.

III. THE END OF THE COLD WAR: IMPETUS FOR DEVELOPMENT EFFORTS?

The change in East–West relations during the last two years – from cold war to co-operation – represents one of the most dramatic effects of the perestroika policy of the USSR leadership under President Gorbachev. What effects may be expected from this change for a more sustainable development in the North and the South? The answer remains hidden in the future; only some opportunities, possibly some probabilities, can be indicated here, leaving aside how lasting the new relationship will be.

The arms race in the North between the East and the West has in the past been seen as a major constraint on development; disarmament and development have been considered as interrelated objectives. Will the end of the cold war free resources for developmental purposes? In that case, where will these resources be diverted to and for what purposes?

It is quite evident that the new international climate, if it continues, will affect the use of public funds for military purposes in the North, although such re-allocations are difficult and will certainly meet with strong resistance. Although the link is not a direct one, it will probably have a similar effect also in the South, where huge military expenditures have constituted an even heavier burden on the budgets, in relative terms, particularly against the background of the glaring poverty and the neglected development tasks of these countries. However, it does not necessarily follow that the use of resources – or skills and manpower – freed by cuts in the defence budgets will be diverted to activities that contribute to a sustainable development; it may even imply the opposite. Assessments of this kind will have to be based on the effects that result from the total use of resources by the countries adapting to the new international environment.

The probability that these resources will be diverted to development in the South – whether sustainable or not – is perhaps even less. The East, which will be confronted by a development crisis of its own in the years to come, will probably be too pre-occupied with the restructuring of its own economies to engage in the South. The probability is that a withdrawal will take place from development engagements that even in the past were modest [*Arefieva, 1990*]. The West will probably, in the decade ahead, give priority to eastern Europe as well; the governments in order to support the political restructuring process, and the private sector, including the transnationals, in pursuance of the expected, longer-term gains. Should this analysis be right, which will depend, *inter alia*, on the evolving stability of these countries, it will lead financial resources and skills to the East; part of these resources might, without the opening up of Eastern Europe, have gone to the South, particularly to the commercially more promising parts. In spite of declarations to the contrary, this is already manifest even with regard to the official development assistance.

There are hopes for more fundamental gains. The threat of an all-out war between East and West, with all its consequences for the planet Earth and humankind, has been reduced. The newly established co-operation between the superpowers may also lead to an agreement banning nuclear tests, although there would need to be more parties to make such a decision effective. The prospects of armed conflicts in the Third World, with devastating consequences for both development and the environment, may also be reduced – in some cases even with immediate effects. The two superpowers, in their search for political influence and strategic positions on a global scale, have in the past given support to the conflicting parties at national and regional levels in the Third World (wars by proxy). In the new situation they may be less inclined to become involved in such conflicts when their more vital interests are not directly involved – and may even withdraw from existing commitments of this kind. This is not to indicate that the primary responsibility for all conflicts in the Third World can be sought in the East–West conflict.

The recent Gulf operation may even indicate an active role by the major powers, including the USSR, in containing future aggressions against international law, thus establishing a new world security order under the auspices of the United Nations. Such expectations will probably be premature; although it is too early for conclusive judgement on lessons learned from this intervention, several factors may indicate that this was a special case unlikely to be frequently repeated. In this particular case two major preconditions for a collective intervention were present: (i) one of the major powers (the US) considered its vital interests threatened by the Iraqi invasion of Kuwait (Saudi Arabia, with its rich oil resources and strong influence on the cost of energy, adapted to US interests, became politically and militarily exposed), and the other main powers did not consider a military intervention to be contrary to their vital interests, on the contrary; and (ii) the resources to meet the costs involved were at hand.

On balance, the developments in eastern Europe and in the USSR itself, resulting from the *glasnost* and *perestroika* policies of the USSR leadership and the disintegration of the East, with nationalism and traditional conflicts in the region coming to the surface anew, remain to be seen.

IV. THE NATIONAL SETTING: THE DECLINING ROLE OF THE STATE VIS-À-VIS THE MARKET

A marked trend during recent years has been the increased role of the market in deciding the turn of economic development, globally (which will be discussed in the next section) and within nation states. A completely free market seldom applies except as a utopian ideology or in textbooks; in the real world, markets are *more* or *less* regulated – by the state or its own actors – and, in most countries, parts of the economy will be exempted from the market and regulated by agreements emerging from negotiations between the involved parties. A free market economy and a planned state economy constitute the two extreme poles between which most national economies are situated. It is the *degree* of intervention by the state *vis-à-vis* the market that matters.

During recent years, particularly during the 1980s, state intervention has been on the decline in the West. Ideologically, a strong lead came from the governments of the US and the UK, where extensive de-regulation took place, including privatisation of parts of the public sector (the UK). However, the ideology did not prevent increasingly protectionist measures *vis-à-vis* competition from outside, particularly by the US administration. The trend towards de-regulation and privatisation affected most Western countries although not to the same extent everywhere. In the East, the planned economies experienced a complete collapse during the same period and these countries are now re-orienting their economies towards the market. The same trend is discernible in the Third World, induced also by the concerted conditionality policy of the International Monetary Fund (IMF), the World Bank and the major bilateral aid donors, involving structural adjustment. However, in these countries, which are characterised by what Gunnar Myrdal has termed the 'soft state' [*Myrdal 1969*], intervention by the state has only exceptionally been particularly strong or efficient, especially *vis-à-vis* the major operators within the private sector, the transnational corporations.

Market forces are probably not suitable to be entrusted with ultimate responsibility for the environment. They have different objectives and priorities (profit making), which may conflict with what serves the commons best, and their time perspective is usually rather short. A weakening of the countervailing power, the intervening state, therefore tends to reduce the prospects of an ecologically sound development.

The state, however, serves as an instrument in the hands of those who hold political power. What matters, therefore, is the type of regime in control – its primary objectives, how its policies can be influenced, and by whom. A strong state with a planned economy can be even more destructive of the environment in pursuance of political and economic objectives that involve huge ecological costs than states with market economies in which the power is less centralised, as is evident from the ecological disasters and human sufferings recently uncovered in eastern Europe and the USSR. A totalitarian, repressive, bureaucratic state has been able to give priority to what it conceived to be good for economic growth at huge negative costs for the environment and the people in the immediate neighbourhood of the projects concerned. However, these disasters can be matched by similar projects at the other end of this scale, caused by some transnational (and national) corporations in search of large and quick profits – at home, but more recently mainly in the Third World, within weak, 'soft' states – with the state as an ally rather than as the countervailing power.

A strong, intervening state therefore emerges as a necessary, but not sufficient, precondition for an ecologically sound development. What matters most is the developmental aims and strategies of the government. Open, democratic societies may give the environment a better chance than societies under repressive, authoritarian rule and a centralised power structure, because the policies and priorities of the former may be influenced by rational arguments and by the people immediately concerned. But democracy in itself is no guarantee of an ecologically sound development. It is not only in the planned economies of the East that economic growth and employment have been sought, centrally and locally, at huge ecological costs; these objectives have also been pursued in the West, with popular support where economic interests or employment opportunities were at stake, as experienced by green activists protesting against ecological damage in local communities.

The main hope is vested in open, democratic societies with mixed economies, where market forces are balanced by an intervening state that makes and enforces the rules of the game – provided environmental concerns are shared by a large part, if not the majority, of the population. Policies are probably most effective and sustainable if agreed upon by those concerned. Environmental concerns are now gaining ever wider and stronger popular support, and governments of different colours, from red to blue, are also increasingly committing themselves to such concerns. Their *will* to meet the costs involved and their *ability* to govern in an ecologically sound way, however, vary extensively.

V. INCREASED GLOBALISATION: MARKET FORCES AND WESTERN CONSUMPTION PATTERNS ARE THE WINNERS

The trend has increasingly been towards globalisation. This applies particularly to the economy but also to culture and politics. Interdependence has been on the increase, although increasing *dependence* may be a better description of the evolving economic relations between the North and the South, excluding parts of the South-East. The dynamics of this process has several sources; scientific and technological advances have probably played the same role in modern times as more advanced weapons played in the past, when new areas were conquered. An important precondition, however, has been a market increasingly relieved of regulations; the predominance of neo-liberal ideologies in the major powers of the West for more than a decade led to increased privatisation and de-regulation and gave more room for the free movement of capital and enterprise across national frontiers.

The main implication is that the market forces – and again, in particular, the large transnational corporations[3] – have increasingly been able to set the course, the priorities and the pace of development almost on a global scale. Recent efforts to extend the rules applied by the General Agreement on Tariffs and Trade (GATT) to services, investments and intellectual property rights will carry this process even further if realised. Internationally, the countervailing powers have been weak; this applies, as noted, in particular to the South, which has mainly experienced the drawbacks – as reflected, for instance, in environmental degradation (polluting industries moving south, over-exploitation of natural resources) without obtaining many advantages in return, being latecomers in the process, again with the exception of the South-East, where a few countries have succeeded even better than most northern countries.

The transition from an agrarian economy based on organic matters to an industrial economy based on matters that are less bio-degradable and are drawing more on non-renewable resources is one of the main sources of the eco-crisis. The globalisation of the economy has added a new dimension. As observed by Johan Galtung [*1990a; 1990b*], nature is depleted at one place, polluted with industrial waste at another, and then polluted with household waste at yet another place, nature being the big loser in what is referred to as a 'developed' or 'modern' economy. The effects are too far removed from the causes, and they do not affect those who take the decisions;[4] a transnational corporation is ideally organised to disperse and dilute responsibility.

Increased globalisation has had a revolutionary impact in our time also on the *cultural* level. One important aspect of this globalisation, made possible by the revolution in communications, is that Western values, norms and ways of life have increasingly crossed frontiers and reached new and large audiences. In the past, some of these frontiers were closed. In the East, the dissatisfaction with the prevailing systems that in the end changed the face of Europe was nurtured by the picture of the affluence and openness of the neighbouring Western societies, transmitted through media which no frontier could stop. In the South, where similiar barriers to a free flow of information existed only in a few cases, the new media and the flow of people and commodities in the wake of the economic penetration transmitted Western life-styles which have probably had a great impact on the course of development aspirations and consumption patterns as well. The main resistance here has come from religious, fundamentalist movements, which only in a few countries of the South have so far been able to influence government policies decisively.

The course of recent developments, in which the cold war has been replaced by co-operation between the superpowers, has, on the *political* level, led to a revival of the United Nations system. In the new international situation, both superpowers seem to see their interest served by giving the UN a larger role in world politics. This changed attitude to the UN was already signalled by President Gorbachev a few years ago [*Gorbachev, 1987*]; now it seems as if the US administration is also willing to give increased attention to this arena anew. However, recent events in the Middle East may have affected this trend.

The position of the South has consistently been in favour of the global system, as was recently confirmed by the South Commission. These governments see their interests as being best served by international regimes and sets of rules which they themselves would be able to influence. Their first major effort to this end came in the mid 1970s, when the aims and a strategy for a new international economic order (NIEO) were formulated and adopted by the UN system. However, in the 1980s, the North–South dialogue came to a virtual standstill. Even so, the main elements of the NIEO policy remain centrally placed in the new development strategy for the South worked out by the South Commission. While environmental concerns were almost totally absent in the NIEO efforts, as noted by Helge Hveem [*1990*], these aspects, as well as the concern for the internal socio-economic and political development in the South (also absent in the NIEO strategy), have been given emphasis by the South Commission [*1990: 7, 279–81*].

The globalisation of the market and of Western life-styles and consumption patterns does not enhance the probability of a more sustainable development in the future. If Western consumption patterns were to be sustained on a global scale, that would presuppose economic growth at a level and with a direction that would involve high environmental costs. The expected population growth only underscores this conclusion. The countervailing powers to the market forces, of which the intervening state seems to be the major one within national boundaries, are much weaker in the international arena, particularly *vis-à-vis* transnational operators that command an arsenal of strategies and means to evade regulations of nation states. The need for a set of rules and an international regime to ensure that environmental concerns are satisfied is glaring; this fact does not, however, imply that the need will be met. It will not be met without concerted efforts by those concerned on all levels, from the local to the global, seeking alliances where trade-offs are possible or different primary objectives can be attained by the same stroke.

VI. THE TREND TOWARDS REGIONALISATION

The trend towards economic and political regionalisation has been evident for some time. This process has, as noted, been particularly strong in the industrially advanced North, but is in the making also in the South-East. Efforts have also been made elsewhere in the South (for instance, in southern Africa (SADCC)), but then at a far less ambitious level and with less effect.

Although this trend may seem to run contrary to the globalisation just discussed, its effects are probably of a similar kind. The main rationale behind these efforts is to give market forces a chance to increase economic growth within a wider space than that of the individual countries involved and to enhance the ability of its private sector (and public enterprises) to compete, inside and outside the region, with competitors based in other northern, industrial countries and in the South-East.

The dynamism in this process is today found in Europe, where the EC is approaching the completion of its internal market next year and is bringing the EFTA countries along into a regional economic space. The recent disintegration of regional co-operation in the East only underscores this dynamism. A large-scale 'internal market' has long been at work in the US and was recently extended by the US–Canadian free trade agreement. The European integration process combines a defensive purpose (protection against competition from North America and the South-East) within the region with an offensive one, maintaining old markets outside the region and conquering new ones. What are the environment and the South in for from this development?

One possible, even probable, scenario has already been indicated, namely that the EC will be an instrument of liberal economic policy, allowing more room for the market forces within the region and providing the basis on which Europe-based and -supported transnational corporations can compete and penetrate the economies in the South and in the East as well, expanding Western life-styles and consumption patterns globally, with effects which have already been discussed. However, other scenarios may also be conceivable. I shall indicate one of these scenarios for an alternative development which may also be possible, even probable, but which guides expectations in a slightly different and more promising direction, at least for the environment, regionally and globally.

The immediate effects of an internal market in Europe – which within a relatively short time span will probably comprise most European countries, directly or indirectly, including those of the East – will be conducive to a free flow of capital, commodities, services and people within the region. While the governments of the EC region will not be able to intervene directly in the way that they could previously within their territories, the free flow will be circumscribed by rules set for the game, which will apply to the whole region (though there will be exceptions). The harmonised rules for environmental protection may, in the initial phase, be less strict than those established at national levels in countries where ecological concerns have been given high priority; the probability is, however, that, in others, the rules will be stricter than before, thus raising the level on a broad, regional basis. This represents a state of affairs at a certain point in time of an ongoing process; as long as this issue receives broad support, from governments and from public opinion, the probability is that the rules will be made stricter over time.

The future course of events cannot be stated today. What, then, are the factors that may indicate a course different from the neo-liberal scenario described above? Although the traditions of European countries differ, the most common pattern in western Europe is that of the mixed market economy, in which the private sector usually predominates, though there is a large public sector – and an intervening state which makes and enforces the rules. In quite a few of these countries, there has been an extensive degree of intervention by the state, and parts of the economy have been governed by agreements to which the state is also a party. Such systems are to be found also outside the north-eastern corner of Europe. Socialist and Social Democratic parties, usually connected with an intervening state, have maintained a strong political position in several countries of western Europe, although at present they are nowhere in a majority position. They are not alone in support of an intervening state, support is also provided by non-Socialist parties, even to the Right, although there may be a difference in emphasis and degree. Strong trade unions tend to pursue a similar course, although, in a conflict between environmental concerns and employment, their positions may be less predictable. Thus, although corporative interests are strong everywhere and well integrated in the state, they are countervailed.

The probability is that this tradition, and the political proponents of an intervening state, will influence the future course of the EC, although not alone. It is still unclear what the countries of eastern Europe may contribute to this process, when life returns to 'normality'. Their peoples have turned down an authoritarian, repressive state and a planned economy; under democratic rule a mixed economy with an intervening state may appear more attractive than the alternatives available.

The EC has established a central planning capacity, an ability to arrive at decisions even involving politically controversial issues, and a political culture which encourages loyalty to the decisions arrived at. Should environmental concerns be given a high priority within the member countries, which is the case at present with several member governments, the Community may be able to enact and follow up a restrictive environmental policy on a regional basis, if necessary, by legal enforcement. If this should be the case, the implications would be much wider. European standards would almost by necessity have an impact on the standards required from prospective exporters to the European market; and the EC would, out of self-interest (in order to preserve the competitiveness of European producers outside the European market), make its weight felt at the global level to push the issue. The EC could, under such circumstances, become a pusher, in the international arenas, for an ecologically more sustainable development.

What can the South expect from the economic and political integration in the EC? The answer will depend on the kind of Europe that will evolve in the years to come. The internal market is a creation of Europeans to serve European interests; however, it does not necessarily follow from this that a 'fortress Europe' will emerge, though it may in some areas. As noted by Louis Emmerij [1990], there is no other actor in the international trading system which has deviated so widely from the principles of free trade as the EC. This applies also to the relations with the Third World, characterised by preferential trading arrangements with a group of Third World countries, historically resulting from the insistence of France in order to maintain, within a wider context, its economic relations with its former colonies. This tradition is reflected in the treaties between the EC and the ACP countries involving trade and aid relations.

Several processes converge as a result of the extensive EC internal market involving some 320 million people and with a GDP of some $2.7 trillion. The market will attract capital from outside, also from the Third World. It will also be attractive to Third World exporters. The preferred group (the African, Caribbean and Pacific countries), which includes most of the poorest and worst off countries, may be expected to be in the best position to benefit from this market. However, the reality may prove to be different. We do not yet know the outcome of the parallel negotiations on Lomé IV and within the GATT; however, if the Uruguay Round of the GATT succeeds in lowering the general level of tariffs, the Third World countries outside the preferred ACP group will be the winners in relative terms. And whatever the level of tariffs, the countries with the best capabilities of producing at competitive prices the kind of products (and possibly services) that are adapted to the tastes and 'needs' in the European market stand the best chance; most ACP countries would not be the front-runners in that race. This applies also to their traditional exports, which, in part, compete with agricultural production within the extended EC and are therefore vulnerable. For all, new 'environmental' standards may add to the effect of such standards as already apply as effective protective measures against imports from Third World countries.

This probable scenario is not a promising one for most Third World countries, particularly the poorest, including most of Europe's traditional partners (the ACP countries). It is not clear how Europe will meet the main challenges of the South Commission. Generous aid will be an important part of such a response, particularly *vis-à-vis* the poorest countries, but will not be a sufficient one. The main arena for hammering out a common strategy, in the short term, is probably the negotiations on Lomé IV. In an increasingly interdependent world, neglect of this issue may involve enormous costs, both in the short and the long term.

VII. THE DEVELOPMENT CRISIS IN THE SOUTH: THE CHALLENGES AHEAD

The South is a problematic concept because the countries in the South vary greatly in size, natural resources, political systems, economic structures, and level of economic, social and technological development. They exhibit wide cultural, religious and ideological variations as well. In the face of this diversity, to expect unity and a common stand on development issues is probably to ask too much. What they have more or less in common, however, is an unfavourable position in the global system, particularly in the world's economic system, with negative effects on their ability to develop. They share a relative poverty *vis-à-vis* the North and, although the internal distribution within some of these countries may be far more unequal than in the North, they also share mass poverty. However, any attempt to generalise is bound to simplify the multifarious variations that exist in the South.

The two or three decades after the Second World War witnessed social and economic progress in many parts of the Third World.[5] In the 1980s, however, the South sank into a deep development crisis. This crisis did not hit all countries equally hard. Some East Asian countries came out well and China and India, both extensive systems and relatively independent of the world economy, accelerated their growth rates; the main losers were the debt-ridden and the commodity-dependent countries, with Sub-Saharan Africa (SSA) coming out worst. The development crisis in the South has several sources and many faces, with variations in different areas. It is related to international economic dependency structures, and the dependency has increased as a result of the crisis. It is also related to the internal policies pursued by Third World governments and, in general, to what can be subsumed under the concept of 'the soft state'. The South is afflicted by an economic crisis, a political crisis, and an ecological crisis. These crises are interrelated.

The magnitude of the debt problem confronting so many Third World countries, though not the original incurring of the debts, results from developments largely outside the control of the borrowing countries, namely the inflation and the dramatic rise in the interest rates in the North, which have made the loans much more expensive than when they were acquired. Servicing the debts has had a devastating effect on the economies of the indebted countries and has led to a negative transfer of resources to the South. Also the rising prices of energy (oil) and capital equipment, on which these countries have made themselves dependent, have contributed to balance-of-payments difficulties. As a result of this, but also as a result of the domestic policies pursued, productivity has been at a low level and is decreasing, in both agriculture and industry. This has affected their foreign economies, with negative effects politically, socially and ecologically.

The *political* crisis is probably most clearly expressed in the widespread disillusion with the state and consequently a decline in its legitimacy, in many Third World countries, particularly in the SSA [*Hydén 1983; Doornbos, 1989*]. Many Third World countries have for years been ruled by authoritarian, often repressive, regimes, but even democratically elected regimes (in the 1980s, a democratisation trend was visible, particularly in Latin America) have encountered the same disillusion, when confronted with expectations that they could not meet under the prevailing economic conditions. The deterioration of public well-being, reflected in such indicators as levels of nutrition, school enrolment, life expectancy and infant mortality, together with massive unemployment, has led to social discontent, protests and political unrest.

The *ecological* crisis in the South is mainly man-made but has also been caused by cyclical natural disasters, like the droughts that hit Sahelian Africa (and elsewhere) with full force during the 1970s and 1980s. Environmental administration is weak everywhere in the South and particularly weak where most needed. The crisis is manifested, *inter alia*, by the desertification and deforestation which have taken place. Many other aspects of the ecological degradation in the South have their roots in the North, as noted. However, stress caused primarily by the massive poverty in the South – increasing in magnitude due to fast-growing populations – makes its own impact.

The challenges – to the South, but also to the North[6] – emerging from this development crisis are formidable. What answers have appeared? In its report, the South Commission [*1990*], headed by Julius K. Nyerere, Tanzania's former President, has made an effort to address this question, recommending development objectives for the South and strategies to attain these objectives. What vision of the future is contained in this report?

Its main vision is a unified world. In order to secure their future, the people of the world 'have now to move towards global unity through widening co-operation on an equitable basis' [*1990: 10*]. The Commission summarises its development perspective as follows [*1990: 13–14*]:

Development is a process of self-reliant growth, achieved through
the participation of the people acting in their own interests as they
see them, and under their own control. Its first objective must be
to end poverty, provide productive employment, and satisfy the
basic needs of all the people, any surplus being fairly shared. This
implies that basic goods and services such as food and shelter, basic
education and health facilities, and clean water must be accessible
to all. In addition, development presupposes a democratic structure
of government, together with its supporting individual freedoms of
speech, organization, and publication, as well as a system of justice
which protects all the people from actions inconsistent with just laws
that are known and publicly accepted.

The Commission gives emphasis to strong economic growth in the South.
However, the consumerist models of the North are rejected. The emphasis
is on the removal of extreme poverty; the development strategies should
aim at 'satisfying basic human needs and at closing the distance between
South and North in food, education, health, safe drinking water, and a
healthy and secure environment' [1990: 273]. Although rapid and sustained
economic growth is seen as a necessity, it is emphasised that economic
growth, as measured by the gross national product, is not synonymous
with development. What matters is what is produced, how and at what
social and environmental cost, by whom and for whom. Development,
as defined,[7] implies growing self-reliance, both individual and collective;
the basis for a nation's development must therefore be its own resources,
fully used to meet its own needs. Development should be people-centred.
It implies political freedom for both individuals and nations – 'the people's
interests and desires can only be known when they are free – and have the
channels – to express them' [1990: 11]. Democratic institutions and popular
participation in decision-making are therefore considered essential.

As summarised above, development strategies are interwoven in the
objectives. Thus, self-reliance emerges both as an objective and a development strategy; this applies also to several of the other objectives, such
as participation, the satisfaction of basic human needs, democratisation
and the ensuring of human rights. Although the level of generalisation
is high and scope is allowed for adaptations, at the country level, to
different national traditions, the recommended course seems very close
to the Social Democratic development model. South–South co-operation
emerges as an essential part of the strategy. Vis-à-vis the North, the main
elements contained in the NIEO programme are maintained, including the
demand for reform of the international system governing the flows of trade,
capital, and technology. As previously, this plea is based on values such

as equity and fairness, although it is recognised that such pleas have not carried the process far since the mid 1970s. There is also an appeal to shared interests, with reference to the environment and health; as poverty constitutes the main cause both of environmental degradation and of threats to health, which no national border can stop, an assault on the poverty in the Third World emerges as a common concern.

These are the main aspirations put forward by some of the most gifted and experienced people of the South. The emphasis is on self-reliance. Where others have recommended de-linking from or confrontation with the North, in which the environmental issue is seen as a trading instrument[8], the Commission gives emphasis to co-operation. Although ideas and visions are indispensable, they seldom change societies, institutions or power relationships overnight. They may, however, inspire political action; as such they are important in creating the future. Their impact will be measured in the follow up in the South. For the more immediate future, there are few signs of an end to the development crisis in the South in its various manifestations. There is little willingness in the North to remove the more immediate constraints on development caused by debts or to address the more fundamental causes of underdevelopment. On the contrary, as stated in the South Commission's own analysis [*1990: 3*], 'domination has been reinforced where partnership was needed and hoped for in the South'. And only a few governments in the South have demonstrated any ability, in the recent past, to pursue the kind of strategy recommended by the South Commission.

VIII. A PRECONDITION FOR SEEING LIGHT AT THE END OF THE
TUNNEL: A FAVOURABLE, ENLIGHTENED PUBLIC OPINION

The prospects for sustainable development may seem bleak, particularly if the kind of economic growth we have experienced, in which market forces exert a strong and even decisive impact on the course of development, is seen as the very root of the ecological crisis.

To expect political, social and economic elites to lead a revolution that will undermine their privileged positions, in order to create a more just society, may appear naive; yet, several leaders of past revolutions have emerged from such elites. A similar contradiction is involved when it is expected that those (particularly in the North, but also in the South) who have become used to an affluent life and familiar with the means to obtain it will freely renounce what they have obtained for the common good; however, some opinion polls have indicated a certain willingness to do so. The magnitude of the problems involved may call for *revolutionary* changes. The most potent source of revolutionary change would be the alternative value systems associated with 'third system' movements [*Friberg and Hettne, 1985; Hettne, 1990*]. However, the most that one can realistically hope for in the foreseeable future is probably *revisions* and modifications of the present course, in which the market forces will be more contained than at present.

Decision-making varies with the political system; different political systems allow different scopes for public participation, competing ideas and interest articulation. What factors may then lead to an ecologically more sustainable development within the more open political systems that seem to be emerging almost on a global scale?

There are no simple answers at hand. The structures in which political, economic and cultural decisions are arrived at are important for the course of events, at both the formal and the informal level. The logic of the structures which are most decisive today is not leading the aspirations and activities of man towards a more ecologically sustainable development, as emphasised above. These structures, however, are man-made and may also be changed by man. In the processes leading to change, whether revolutionary or revisionist, a concerned and active civil society is a *sine qua non* – and the multi-faceted 'third system' is among the main agents.

The evolving *public opinion* will therefore be decisive. Attitudes are formed as much by basic norms and value systems as by interests. They are fed by information and knowledge; ideas and insight become of crucial importance. The most important contribution of the research community may, therefore, be to generate new and well-founded insights into the processes at work and their effects on the environment; the consequences of different development models would be of particular interest and importance.

The evolving *norms*, at all levels, will also be decisive. Sustainable development, on the global scale, has to be based on some kind of international solidarity – or *humane internationalism* [*Pratt, 1989, 1990; Stokke, 1989*] – as different areas of the world will emerge differently from the ecological changes that take place. The main (neo-liberal) trend in the recent past does not give much promise for the immediate future.

Another important challenge for research will be to generate new knowledge on which future growth, within the confines of an ecologically sound development, can be based. For the political authorities, the challenge is to create the organisational and financial conditions necessary to mobilise creativity in this direction, using the carrot as well as the stick (setting standards, using regulatory powers).

NOTES

1. The concepts used are too broad to capture a reality rich in variations; even worse, they may be misleading. The reference is mainly to some major economic systems, in a broad sense, that may or may not involve organised political and/or military co-operation. Other concepts at a similarly aggregate level in common use may be more helpful, although they also are captives of the fallacies of general concepts. Thus, 'West' (and 'North-West') refer basically to the OECD countries (the industrially more advanced, market-oriented countries of the North), including Japan, which does not fit into the geographical concept (nor into its cultural connotation). 'South-East', with reference to co-operation in the making within a *geographical* region, used here but not in common use, includes Japan as the core power, although it belongs geographically to the North and is a prominent member of the OECD. In this region, several countries have recently attained a high level of industrialisation and have managed to become successful competitors with the old industrial world within a 'global' market system.

2. This is recognised by the South Commission [*1990: 272*], which maintains that most developing countries will need to expand their economies at a fairly rapid rate to satisfy the legitimate aspirations of their peoples. 'The South needs strong economic growth, including advances in both agriculture and industry, to provide a decent livelihood for all those entering the labour market. This process of growth will entail a significant increase in the use of natural resources, to which the international community will have to adjust if the South is to attain its development goals without harming global ecological stability.'

3. Paul Ekins [*1990: 11*] considers the transnational corporation a counter-trend to the spread of the global market. 'The largest corporations now have a higher turnover than most countries. In terms of structure they resemble nothing so much as the former command-and-control economies of Eastern Europe and the Soviet Union which have now acquired such a bad name: within them resources are allocated through hierarchical dictat rather than by market forces. These giant corporations therefore represent great islands of central planning within the global market. Moreover, because of their economic power, they are able greatly to broaden the range of price-setting possibilities, including transfer-pricing, predatory pricing, oligopolistic pricing, etc.'

4. Johan Galtung [*1990b*] emphasises the role of the civil society in achieving a development oriented towards basic human needs for all, in equitable, peaceful, participatory national and global societies in ecological balance. Thus, voluntary organisations may, *inter alia*, monitor the ecological state-of-affairs not only at the receiving end (at home, at work) but also at the sending end (at factory outlets); may contract economic-ecological cycles by re-establishing the link between the evil-doer and the evil consequences; may be willing to adapt dramatic measures that not only hit the economy but also civil society; and may adopt ever higher levels of consciousness and conscience in market behaviour. None of these excludes the many valuable ideas of the Brundtland Commission, but they are 'people-based, more local and place people's fate more in their own hands – where it should be.'

5. However, the relative gap between the North and the South did not narrow and the absolute gap widened. As argued by Frances Stewart [*1990*], the flows of capital and technology from the North to the South were associated with increasing dependence of the South on the North. 'Northern ownership of Southern industry was rising through the expansion of multilateral companies; the South was paying a heavy price for the technology; aid flows were argued to be accompanied by decreasing domestic saving and did not raise but even reduced growth; Southern dependence on primary product exports was largely maintained as a result of Northern trade restrictions; commodity price trends – if not as unambiguously bad as predicted by Prebisch – showed considerable fluctuations and offered poor absolute terms of trade, in "unequal exchange". All-in-all, it was widely suggested, colonialism had been displaced by neo-colonialism.' Moreover, the aggregate growth rates in southern economies 'were accompanied by increasing impoverishment; growth was failing to "trickle down" to the poor, because of the capital-intensity of technology, growing inequalities in asset distribution and the neglect of basic needs.'

6. Professor Rehman Sobhan, Director of the Bangladesh Institute of Development Studies, observes quite crisply [Sobhan, 1990] that it is fortunate for the countries of the North that it took some two centuries for our ecological conscience to be aroused. 'During the 19th and most of the 20th century they have happily destroyed the forest cover of most of Europe and North America, made extinct the bison and innumerable other species of flora and fauna, polluted their rivers into noisome sewers where to take a swim is to risk one's life, polluted their skies and atmosphere and have now laid siege to the stratosphere. Having ravaged nature quite comprehensively in their own lands they moved into the Third World whose natural resources were plundered, its native cultures, society, economy and ecology destabilised and contemporary generations, now integrated into a global market, compelled to sustain this assult on their nature for their survival.' The unanswered question for the Third World remains, who will pay the costs of depreciating the ecological inheritance of mankind? 'The North having had its share of the cake and being unwilling to pay the historic cost of this share, can make few moral or legal claims on the South.'

7. 'Development is a process which enables human beings to realize their potential, build self-confidence, and lead lives of dignity and fulfilment. It is a process which frees people from the fear of want and exploitation. It is a movement away from political, economic, or social oppression. Through development, political independence acquires its true significance. And it is a process of growth, a movement essentially springing from within the society that is developing' [1990: 10].

8. Paul Ekins [1990] argues that a concern for sustainability profoundly alters the basic North–South relationship because of the interdependencies in the global environment; it gives the South a stronger hand in the negotiations. However, he makes a distinction between those environmental issues on which Southern action can have a decisive impact on northern life-styles (climatic change, including global warming, and ozone depletion) and other issues which affect Southern countries less interdependently (desertification, soil erosion, water depletion, toxic waste exports, etc.), indicating that Northern governments put a low priority on Southern environments per se.

REFERENCES

Arefieva, Elena B., 1990, 'Soviet Perestroika and the New Aid Policy', Paper presented at the 6th EADI General Conference in Oslo, June 1990.

Doornbos, M.R., 1989, 'The African State in Academic Debate', Dies Natalis 1989, The Hague: Institute of Social Studies.

Ekins, Paul, 1990, 'Sustainability: Mutuality and Conflict in North–South', Paper presented at the EADI 6th General Conference in Oslo, June 1990.

Emmerij, Louis J., 1990, 'Europe 1992 and the Developing Countries: Conclusion', Journal of Common Market Studies, Vol.XXIX, No.2 (Dec.)

Friberg, Mats and Björn Hettne, 1985, 'The Greening of the World – Towards a Non-Deterministic Model of Global Processes', Development As Social Transformation, London: Hodder & Stoughton.

Galtung, Johan, 1990a, 'Goals and Processes of Development. An Integrated View', Forum for utviklingsstudier, 1990: 1, Oslo: Norwegian Institute of International Affairs (NUPI).

Galtung, Johan, 1990b, 'Beyond Brundtland: Linking Global Problems and Local Solutions', Paper presented at the EADI 6th General Conference in Oslo, June 1990.

Gorbachev, Mikhail, 1987, 'Security in the World: Reality and Guarantees', in Pravda and Izvestija, 17 Sept. 1987.

Hardin, G., 1968, 'The Tragedy of the Commons', Science, 162.

Helland, Johan, 1990, 'Finding a New Sustainable Pastoralism or Sustaining Pastoralists', Forum for utviklingsstudier, 1990:2, Oslo.

Hettne, Bjørn, 1990, Development Theory and the Three Worlds, London: Longman.

Hveem, Helge, 1990, 'Missing Link? North–South Relations and Sustainable Development', *Forum for utviklingsstudier*, 1990: 1, Oslo.

Hydén, Göran, 1983, *No Shortcuts to Progress: African Development Management in Perspective*, Berkeley CA: University of California Press.

Myrdal, Gunnar, 1969, *Asian Drama: An Inquiry into the Poverty of Nations*, New York: Twentieth Century Fund and Pantheon Books.

NAVF, 1990, Final Summary Statement from the Conference on Sustainable Development, Science and Policy, Bergen, 8–12 May 1990, Oslo: Norwegian Research Council for Science and the Humanities.

Pratt, Cranford (ed.), 1989, *Internationalism under Strain*, Toronto: University of Toronto Press.

Pratt, Cranford (ed.), 1990, *Middle Power Internationalism. The North–South Dimension*, Kingston: McGill-Queen's University Press.

Sobhan, Rehman, 1990, 'Third World Perspectives on Priorities for Sustainable Development', Paper presented at the EADI 6th General Conference in Oslo, June 1990.

South Commission, 1990, *The Challenge to the South*, Oxford: Oxford University Press.

Stewart, Frances, 1990, 'The Role of the South in a Chaotic World', Paper presented at the EADI 6th General Conference in Oslo, June 1990.

Stokke, Olav (ed.), 1989, *Western Middle Powers and Global Poverty: The Determinants of the Aid Policies of Canada, Denmark, the Netherlands, Norway and Sweden*, Uppsala: Scandinavian Institute of African Studies.

WCED, 1987, *Our Common Future*, Oxford/New York: Oxford University Press.

Sustainable Development:
The Challenges Ahead

Gro Harlem Brundtland*

The question of how we should deal with change – and how we can promote it – is of great concern to politicians and to scientists alike. Both professions must be able to analyse the lessons of the past, they must perceive the transformations of the present and they must judge the prospects for the future.

When the World Commission on Environment and Development (WCED) embarked in its task of drawing up 'a global agenda for change', I was very much aware of the need to put together a highly qualified political and scientific team. We needed input from both disciplines to fulfil the task assigned us by the General Assembly.

The report 'Our Common Future' based its analysis on the best available scientific knowledge about the state of our global environment and the direct link between environment and development. The picture which emerged was deeply disturbing. Forests are vanishing. Every year, about 150.000 km^2 disappear, and the latest indicators show that the destruction of tropical rain forests is even more widespread than we feared. In the process, individual species are disappearing at a highly alarming rate, affecting biological diversity. This is irreversible change, and it is occurring at a rate never before witnessed on this planet, undermining the potential for development.

Deserts are spreading at a yearly rate of about 60,000 km^2, consuming vast tracts of agricultural land. Soil erosion is continuing at an accelerating pace, further reducing the area that can be used for food production for a rapidly growing world population.

Our understanding of global environmental change has been revolutionised in recent years. But even as we amass scientific knowledge in greater quantities than ever before, we still know too little about the long-term effects of present trends. The pace of change is simply outstripping the ability of scientific disciplines to assess and advise.

As scientists, you are very well aware that our conclusions and

---

*Chairman of the World Commission on Environment and Development (WCED) and now the Prime Minister of Norway. Keynote speech at the 6th EADI General Conference in Oslo, 27 June 1990.

predictions are most uncertain in areas where several variables interact with each other. But in our struggle to save the global environment, we must make increasing use of interdisciplinary approaches. Not only will we have to deal increasingly with linkages between different disciplines of science. We will also need to know much more about how these changes interact with the economic system. Advances in various sectors during this century – in science and technology, in industry, energy, agriculture and forestry – have resulted in fundamental changes both in our economies and in our environment. As pointed out by the World Commission, economy and ecology are becoming increasingly interwoven, locally, regionally, nationally and globally – in a seamless web of cause and effect.

How to deal with scientific uncertainty caused by rapid change was one of the many important topics discussed at the Bergen Conference in May 1990. I am encouraged by the consensus finally reached among the Ministers on the precautionary principle. It was an important step forward that Ministers of the 34 Economic Commission of Europe countries were able to agree that the criterion of full scientific certainty should not be used to postpone measures to prevent environmental degradation. Environmental measures must anticipate, prevent and attack the causes of environmental degradation.

I believe the input from the Science Conference in Bergen was instrumental in achieving this consensus. The scientists argued convincingly that it will be better to have been roughly right in due time than precisely right too late. The Science Conference also identified important criteria for international action which will be used long after the Bergen Conference. When environmental changes are global in scale, irreversible and transgenerational, anticipatory assessments aimed at narrowing uncertainties and estimating the type and magnitude of effects are particularly needed. In such cases, early intervention by policy-makers may be crucial to prevent costly harm.

The World Commission concluded that it would be futile to deal with the symptoms of global ecological degradation if we do not at the same time attack the problem at its roots. This means committing ourselves to a cooperative effort to deal with the problems of world poverty, uneven development and population growth.

World poverty remains a main cause and effect of environmental degradation. Those who are poor will continue to destroy their immediate environment in order to survive. Their livestock will overgraze grasslands, they will overuse marginal land, and they will crowd into congested cities in ever growing numbers. We know a lot about such processes; yet there is a need for more knowledge about the multiple links between poverty and environmental degradation.

The international response to 'Our Common Future' has been encouraging in many respects:

- We have made significant progress in raising public awareness and drawing political attention to the need for urgent action.
- There is now much broader participation in our efforts, from international organisations, from national governments, from the scientific community, from a broad spectre of voluntary organisations and environmental groups and from individual citizens.
- Our primary diagnosis, that environmentally sound and sustainable development is essential for our planetary survival, has been almost universally accepted.
- Our call for sustainable development as the only viable strategy for the management of global change has been widely adopted.

The task now – three years after the World Commission submitted its report – is to define how to continue the process of translating the call for sustainable development into concrete action, how to build truly global co-operation and how to establish the necessary mechanisms for technological and financial transfers needed to combat environmental degradation and poverty in the Third World.

On vital areas of concern, there is little cause for optimism, however. The efforts to combat poverty and improve living conditions in the Third World have gone backwards rather than forwards. The tragic reversal in the flow of financial resources from the poor countries to the rich, propelled by the debt crisis, continues.

Perhaps most dangerous of all, we have made very little progress in our efforts to curb world population growth. In the 1990s, we shall have our last chance to prevent another doubling of the world's population. If population growth is not slowed by declining birth rates, it will be slowed by famine or malnutrition. Let us not forget that this is also a question of women's rights and roles, of basic needs, of the right to education, family planning and a decent life.

The EADI conference has been convened on the general theme of new challenges for European Development Research. It will address two subjects, developments in Europe and sustainable development, both of which will have an important impact on a third, that is, North–South relations. These issues are, of course, closely interrelated. There is now much concern in the developing world that the increased attention focused on the situation in Central and Eastern Europe will divert financial and technological resources from the Third World.

Some of this concern is clearly justified. During the last 12 months, the pace of events in Europe has been such that it has required the full attention of policy-makers. We have seen concrete examples that funds earmarked for the developing countries have been used to finance aid programmes for the democracies emerging in the East. It was an important confidence-building measure from the countries of the North that the Ministerial Declaration from the Bergen Conference stated that assistance to Eastern Europe for environmental purposes should not reduce our aid to the developing countries.

All European nations must now join forces in a committed, dedicated effort to halt ecological decline on the European continent. Sustainable development must become an integral part of the economic reconstruction of Europe. We must use the opportunities available to us to transfer some of the enormous scientific and technological resources which have been used for military purposes into environment and development. The peace dividend must become a sustainable development dividend.

The extent of the environmental damage in Central and Eastern Europe is dramatic. The estimates of how much it will cost to repair the damage done are staggering. Nevertheless, we have reason to be hopeful that the European nations together can reverse present negative trends. We have the financial resources. We have the scientific knowledge and an unprecedented potential for technological innovation. We are witnessing a new political will, nurtured by pressure from a public opinion which is becoming increasingly concerned with the ways things now are going. Through a new European Economic Space encompassing the EC and EFTA countries, through a strengthened CSCE and an invigorated ECE, through the European Environment Agency and the European Bank for Reconstruction and Development, we will soon also have the organizational capability to make rehabilitation of the natural environment on the European continent an integral part of the effort to create a new Europe.

But there would be little use in winning that battle if we lose the overall war to reverse global degradation. In the next two years, as the preparations for the 1992 World Conference on Environment and Development in Brazil proceed, we must refocus our attention on the challenges to our global environment. The most global – and potentially the most serious – of all the issues facing us today, is how we should deal with the threats to the world's atmosphere. According to the most authoritative scientific assessment of climate change ever produced, the Intergovernmental Panel on Climate Change, scientists are now certain that the increased emissions of greenhouse gases will enhance the greenhouse effect, resulting in additional warming of the surface of the earth. We can expect major changes in the global distribution of wind, rainfall and temperature. The direct effects of climatic change will have powerful economic, social and political consequences for the world community.

Scientists cannot today predict with any degree of certainty the magnitude or the distribution of the expected climate change. But even if the lowest estimates of global warming prove true, climate change will occur faster than at any time before in human history. We are entering an age of the unknown, where we may be in for some very unwelcome surprises. And even though our knowledge of the earth's ecology is quickly expanding, we do not know enough to say with certainty how much the system as a whole can tolerate or what its capacity may be for sustaining human development.

Several negotiating processes are now under way to deal with the threats to the atmosphere. An important agreement was reached in London in June 1990 on the establishment of a financial mechanism to help developing countries reduce their use of chemicals which erode the ozone layer. After the presentation of the IPCC report, the next step will be negotiations on a World Climate Convention. While a general framework convention could possibly be negotiated fairly quickly, the efforts to reach truly effective international measures to combat global warming will be among the most difficult, and most important, thus far in the brief history of global politics.

An effective climate convention would have to deal with the problem of CO_2 emissions and of other greenhouse gases. At the Bergen Conference in June 1990 and after, we have seen a growing commitment among European nations to at least stabilise CO_2 emissions during the coming decade. But we also know that stabilization at present levels would be highly insufficient if we want to reduce the risk of dramatic climate change. We need to move beyond that, to fairly drastic cuts in emissions early in the next century.

To achieve such changes, we need to deal squarely with the energy issue, which today is not regulated by any kind of global agreements. Today, energy consumption releases more than five billion tons of carbon into the atmosphere each year. Worldwide energy demand increases even as our knowledge of how energy use threatens the global environment grows. To make matters even more complicated, we are starting from a situation in which world energy consumption is highly unequitable. One-fifth of the world's population today consumes more than 70 per cent of the world's commercial energy.

In our energy-intensive industrialised societies, new technologies for energy saving have already slowed the growth rates of energy use. The amount of energy needed to produce one unit of gross national product fell by one fifth between 1973 and 1985. We need to move much faster in reducing our use of those energy forms which damage the environment:

- We need to move towards sustainable energy policies, both at the national and at the global level. Present energy policies in effect subsidise environmental destruction. Such changes will have to come through the political process, and this will require a change of attitude in those countries which have resisted such energy policies in the past.
- We must use the mechanisms of the market, letting the price of energy reflect its true environmental costs, both at production and consumption levels. At present, falling energy prices encourage neither energy conservation nor increased efficiency. The signal from the market is that energy is cheap, freely available and can be used at leisure. This is untenable from an environmental point of view, and the situation should be corrected as quickly as possible in line with the commitment from Bergen.
- We must encourage the emergence of new technologies which can help us to save energy, or make energy use more environmentally clean. Such technologies exist already, and technological ingenuity can further enable us to operate our societies at much lower energy levels than today.
- We should step up our research efforts to develop alternative energy sources, such as solar or wind power.

The true test of our ability to achieve sustainable development at the global level will come in developing countries, where the most rapid growth in energy consumption is now taking place. Developing countries will need more, not less energy for their future development. Even dramatic improvements in energy efficiency will not be sufficient to protect the environment if they are confined to the industrialised world. Unless we find ways to convince developing countries that the curbing of energy-related emissions is compatible with growth and development, it will be very difficult for them to sign a World Climate Convention.

Better terms for the transfer of technology and additional financial resources have become keywords for the developing countries in today's negotiations on global environment issues. Both demands are highly justified and should be supported. Yet, we are today far from an international consensus on the necessity of urgent action, on the targets which should be set for our efforts, and on the international mechanisms which will enable us to reduce global emissions soon enough to avoid the high-risk scenarios of future climate change.

We need to mobilise all the innovative capacity in the political and scientific communities to find new approaches to meet the challenge. A special effort is needed to find financial mechanisms which will make it possible for the developing world to join the global effort.

If we look at the way traditional North–South negotiations have been dragging on in the last 20 years, it is easy to be pessimistic about the prospects of success. But we cannot afford to give up or to lose hope. What we need is a general mobilisation of our collective resources, both in the public and the private sectors, to direct the world economy onto tracks that would make it truly sustainable.

The Science Conference in Bergen made several points very clear:

– Within an action programme to eliminate Third World debt in exchange for sustainable development investments, and reform of trade barriers to support similar aims, we need a better understanding of the mechanisms that determine international economic relations. This will involve research on how trade conventions can be adjusted gradually to close the opportunity gap between developed and developing countries.
– The effect of aid, trade and economic and technological developments in industrialised countries on resource use and the physical environment in developing countries should be taken up as a priority research area for co-operation between scientists in the North and South.
– Governments and scientific institutions share a major responsibility with regard to supporting the build-up of scientific competence on environmental issues in the developing world. This should be done through transfer of funds to support specific Third World environmental change centres, as well as through extensive scientific exchange programmes between North and South.

Scientific and political efforts must both contribute to necessary change. Political leadership at the highest levels will be called for. The CSCE summit in November 1990 put the new threats to our security high on the European agenda for the 1990s. The 1992 World Conference in Brazil should be a global summit, drawing up a strategy to reverse ecological degradation in the 1990s and beyond.

We need to combine political commitment from the top with the enthusiasm which can be mobilised at the grass roots and individual levels. Sustainable development is a participatory process. The spread of democracy and pluralism in the world, with greater emphasis on transparency and the people's right to know, is a necessary and highly welcome boost to our efforts. The broad participation of the scientific community, industry, trade unions, youth and environmental groups which was achieved through the Bergen process should also be part of the preparatory process for Brazil. Other groups, such as women's groups and religious organisations, should be allowed to take part. The scientific community will have a particularly important role to play in these efforts, and I am pleased to see the proposal from the Science Conference in Bergen regarding the holding of a Global Science Summit as part of the preparations for the 1992 conference.

We need institutional reform at both the regional and the global level to improve the efficiency of present decision-making mechanisms on issues which are vital for sustainable development. Narrow definitions of national self-interest or self-reliance become meaningless when the survival of life on our planet is at stake. I am convinced that we will have to find ways to establish stronger international institutions to deal with such issues, possibly with supranational authority for decision-making, monitoring and ensuring compliance. We need a strengthened United Nations to deal forcefully with the vital issues of the next century.

We need to employ a broad array of economic instruments, both incentives and disincentives, to increase the efficiency of energy protection. Regulatory approaches, defined by accountable governments, will continue to be a key element in our efforts. Environmental taxes on environmentally damaging activities and products or energy-wasting products will be needed. Subsidies should be reduced or eliminated wherever they encourage activities which are environmentally harmful. Emission charges or fees, tradeable permits and tax incentives should also be considered.

We will continue to need official development assistance, and we should continue to argue for true additions to present efforts. But traditional ODA will not be enough. We should consider establishing supplementary sources of revenue for international funds for environment and development, for instance through a more direct link with environmental fees collected at national levels.

We must find new and more cost-effective methods of curbing pollution and other harmful activities. The present means of arriving at international environmental agreements, based on the principle of equal percentage reductions for each participatory nation, is not cost-effective. It promotes clean-up in those countries which can afford to invest in new environmental technologies or cleaner industrial plants. At the same time, poorer nations may be unable to live up to their international obligations or to take part in environmental agreements at all, even though the marginal cost of a clean-up may be much lower than in more developed countries. We need to target our efforts to get the maximum environmental value for our money, regardless of where the money is used.

We need more knowledge about how we can achieve the right blend of economic approaches. Measures which may be appropriate for one country in the North may not be the right approach for the nations in the South. The mechanisms of the market should be used to promote sustainable industry and green consumerism in market economies, but such strategies would be of little use in countries where market economies have not yet been established. For development to be sustainable, it must be based on processes that are efficient, equitable, and environmentally sound. But they must also be endogenous if they are to match the aspirations of the people with the resources available to them.

We need to develop sustainable development indicators – a new kind of SDI – which can better reflect the true state of economic and environmental resources. National income accounting must be supplemented with statistics which also reflect the importance of natural resources as depletable or renewable economic assets. We should continue our efforts to elaborate the human dimension of development, such as the recent study published by the UNDP.

Above all, we need to generate growth, particularly in poor nations. Many have been sceptical about the call of the World Commission for new economic growth. But we believe such growth to be absolutely necessary to combat the poverty and devastation that is on the rise in much of the developing world. This growth must be based on policies which sustain and expand the environmental resource base. The concept and quality of growth must be changed.

That is why it is crucial for development researchers to intensify their efforts in connection with the economics of sustainability, as many of you are doing in your work. We need to know more about the linkage between technological advance and economic growth in industrialised countries, and economic development in the South. We need to know how to ensure that sustainable development in Europe will lead not only to improvements in the quality of life in our region, but also be of direct benefit to the developing world. Otherwise, it will not be sustainable at the global level.

We need to know more about how to supply food for a world population which will perhaps be twice as large as today. Agriculture has been the dominant agent of land transformation for centuries. It is a key to sustainable development, particularly in developing countries. Even today, local food production is being outstripped by population growth in many countries in the Third World. At the global level, food supplies may already become precarious within the next five years, as environmental degradation threatens production potential and demand increases.

We need better information systems to analyse the interaction between environmental, economic, social, demographic and bio-physical trends of rural livelihood systems. We need more sustainable agricultural policies at every level. We need to devise a better, more equitable system of world trade in agricultural products, while respecting the need of individual countries to maintain their production potential.

We must continue our work, both among politicians and scientists, on the more traditional elements of development policies, such as the debt crisis and the population issue. They are all vital not only to development, but also to our struggle to save the global environment.

The massive reversal of the flow of resources from the South to the North is taking a heavy toll, not only on the population in developing countries, but also on the environment itself. Tropical rain forests are being cut down at a reckless rate, mineral deposits are being overexploited, vulnerable soil is being put to the plough – all to pay foreign debt. Present strategies to meet the debt crisis are not working well, and we need new ideas as to how the problem should be tackled. Debt relief must continue to be part of our efforts. The idea of debt-for-nature-swaps could also be explored further, although I sympathise with some of the misgivings that have been voiced in the developing world about this particular kind of arrangement.

The population issue will continue to be vital to our efforts to stop global ecological degradation. We know the main factors responsible for population growth. Poverty is one crucial factor, the situation of women is another, cultural and religious conditions constitute a third set of factors. We need to continue studies on how these factors interact and how they affect the size of families. And we certainly need to strengthen international institutions dealing with family planning and population issues. Given the magnitude of the problem and its enormous implications for the future of our planet, present efforts are pitifully inadequate.

Most of the problems I have discussed will be on both the political and the scientific agendas during the 1990s. In the years ahead, the scientists will be seated beside the diplomats and the politicians at the international negotiating tables. Scientific groups have played a major part in the effort to save our environment from the very beginning. We will continue to need your advice and your assistance in mobilising the vast scientific and technological resources which exist in the world community today in a committed, co-operative effort to achieve sustainable development, and to secure Our Common Future.

Environmental Sustainability with Development: What Prospects for a Research Agenda?

Harold Brookfield*

PURPOSE AND PROBLEM

This is an article with a pragmatic objective, that of suggesting ways in which a meaningful research agenda in development studies, contributing toward sustainability, can be delineated. This implies a focus on research at the scale of nations, regions and places, and especially at the lower end of the range. In order to approach this question, it is however first necessary to consider global issues, and in particular the meaning to be given to the elusive concept of 'sustainability'.

Without apology, I concentrate almost entirely on 'environmental sustainability', on the premise that the practice of development, especially but not only in the Third World, depends ultimately on the continued viability of the resource base. I also concentrate on the land-based resource aspect of the problem, and on rural issues, which are my own areas of specialism as a geographer concerned with rural change. However, the goals of development concern people, and the condition of the urban poor is closely linked with that of rural society. I agree entirely with Pearce *et al.* [*1990: 2–3*] that sustainable development must be measured by progress along a vector made up of attributes that include improvement in income and its distribution, in health, education, freedoms, and access to resources. Or, as they put it elsewhere [*Pearce et al., 1989: 2*], it requires that 'real incomes rise, that educational standards increase, that the health of the nation improves, that the general quality of life is advanced'. I also agree with them that the stock of natural capital is the essential basis of such progress. This, however, is where the problem arises, for there is a quite large school (or schools) of thought, including some very respected thinkers

*Division of Society and Environment, Research School of Pacific Studies, The Australian National University, Canberra. The author is particularly grateful to his research assistant, Yvonne Byron, for an inspired job of search among a particularly incoherent literature, and to his colleagues in the ANU, Douglas Porter, Michael Common and Bryant Allen, for valuable comments on a first draft. The article was delivered as a paper in an abbreviated form at the Oslo conference of EADI on 28 June 1990.

on sustainability issues, who believe that a 'sustainable development' that involves continued growth is itself a contradiction, since the only true sustainability demands cessation of growth, and major reconstruction of the whole global economy along conservationist lines. An article concerned with the implications of 'sustainability' for development research cannot avoid facing this basic incompatibility. I face it on the ground chosen by most of the literature, which is that of a fairly predictable natural world system; only later do I introduce the reality of major and increasing uncertainties.

THE EMERGENCE OF 'SUSTAINABLE DEVELOPMENT'

Sustainability, Environmental Economics and Development

The modern emphasis on sustainable utilisation of resources is traced by O'Riordan [*1988: 36*] to a series of African-based conferences in the 1960s, and the discussions around the World Environment Conference in Stockholm in 1972. However, it was the World Conservation Strategy [*IUCN, 1980*] that first brought the concept into prominence. The collision of ideas is between 'development as growth', as East and West alike have pursued it most of this century, and realisation that the resultant plunder and degradation of resources threaten inter-generational equity. It is argued that the resources and capacities of a finite world are, notwithstanding all of human inventiveness, the ultimate 'scarce good' [*Daly and Cobb, 1989: 116*]. Such issues are not new to economic thinking, going back indeed to the classical economists, but belief in the creation of value only by either labour or by utility obscured them. Martinez-Alier [*1987*] has traced the failure of the laws of thermodynamics, and particularly the notion of entropy, to make any serious mark on economic thinking before the time of Georgescu-Roegen's [*1971*] demarche.

Modern resource economics has, in the main, continued to echo Hotelling's [*1931*] opposition to the conservationist views of his day, which Hotelling regarded as playing into the hands of monopolists. While resource exhaustibility clearly called for an economic calculus of its own, short- and medium-term exhaustibility has itself been called into question, in part because of the possibilities for substitution [e.g. *Barnett and Morse, 1963; Kemp et al., 1984*]. A major discussion by Fisher [*1981: 10–89*] developed a modern fashion by seeking theories of 'optimal depletion' of non-renewables, and 'optimal use' of renewable resources, a fashion echoed in more recent work cited below. A wave of more alarmed new thinking arose in the context of the emergent modern environmental movement of the 1960s [*Boulding, 1966*]. The subsequent growth of an emergent environmental stream in economics has certainly not followed any one single approach [e.g. *Bohm and Kneese (eds.), 1971; Solow, 1971; 1974; Lecomber, 1975; Pearce, 1976; Kneese, 1977; Mishan, 1977; Daly, 1977; 1980; 1984; 1988; Baumol and Oates, 1979; Fisher, 1981; Perrings, 1987; Turner (ed.), 1988; Daly and Cobb, 1989; Underwood and King, 1989; Pearce and Turner, 1990; Pearce et al., 1990*]. A majority view has simply been that the price system, together with some controls aided by fiscal measures, can be used to guide growth in less harmful ways. However, most writers have insisted on the impossibility of continued rapid economic growth based on unchecked consumption of resources, and a minority group has argued that the only sustainable future lies in a 'steady-state' economy in dynamic balance with the processes of the biosphere. The latter group, with its elitist and impractical denial of growth, could hardly have been expected to have an impact on either the theory or practice of economic development. However, it is more surprising that the environmental stream as a whole has made so little mark. Perhaps this is at least in part because most of the literature has conducted its argument around certain issues of greatest concern in the wealthier industrialised nations, and has until very lately virtually ignored Third World poverty and distress.

As is commonly the case when different intellectual camps stand apart, each holds some part of the whole truth. The development drive, for all its uneasy and turbulent mix of the Hayek-through-Friedmann tradition, Keynesianism, and Stalinist state planning, has recognised throughout the need to create wealth in order that it may be redistributed; in principle, if not always in practice, it has pursued an altruistic social goal. However, it is not wholly unfair to say that it has tended to assume that intervention to secure 'development' is the responsibility and prerogative of the State, even if the role of the State is simply to give free rein to the 'market'; the 'externalities'are absorbed by the civil society and are thus someone else's concern. The environment is such an externality. I tacitly accepted such a view myself in a critical review of development thinking down to the early 1970s [*Brookfield, 1975*]; the dimension that then seemed to me to be missing was spatial, not environmental. Even down to the mid-1980s, most development theorists have remained deaf to a large literature that since the 1950s, even the 1920s, has warned of the evils of erosion, desertification, resource degradation, pollution and the destruction of amenity that Third World development has created. This applies even to otherwise excellent reviews of trends and counter-trends in development theory and practice, such as those of Apthorpe and Krahl [*1986*] and Toye [*1987*]. Two years ago I discussed this intellectual gap in general terms [*Brookfield, 1988*]; now I must become more precise, and more constructive.

Emergence of Wider Environmental Concern

The environmentally aware stream outside development economics also has a long intellectual pedigree. The basic notion that 'growth' is ultimately unsustainable goes back to Mill [*1848*], if not very much further back in time as Glacken [*1967*] and Passmore [*1974*] have indicated. The widespread consequences of deforestation for agriculture and timber exploitation were clearly and effectively demonstrated in the 19th century by Marsh [1864], and by a whole group of writers whose work effectively brought about important transformations of land use in the Alps. Even Engels [*1876/1970, 3: 74–5*] penned an uncharacteristic passage which warned of the revenge taken by nature for human 'victories', and of 'the more immediate and the more remote consequences of our interference with the traditional course of nature'. Earlier in this century, however, environmentalism remained largely confined to the industrialised countries of Europe and North America, and some late-colonial attempts to preach and enforce its doctrines in the Third World aroused more than just resentment; they even fed rebellion.

After the 1972 Stockholm conference, the compromise view that development and conservation must go hand in hand gained wider currency in the Third World, though without much immediate sense of urgency [e.g. *Ul Haq, 1976: 117–21*]. In the 1970s and early 1980s some social development theorists began to write in terms of 'ecodevelopment' [e.g. *Sachs, 1976; Riddell, 1981; Sachs, 1984; Glaeser (ed.), 1984*]. This approach combined basic needs, at that time the buzzword of development economics, with self-reliance and, above all, environmental compatibility. The 'world conservation strategy' [*IUCN, 1980*] carefully gave a dual emphasis to the relief of poverty and to ecological sustainability, but the effect was small. In the aftermath of the Brundtland report [*World Commission, 1987*], this 'dialogue of the deaf' seems at last to be at an end. 'Sustainable development' now carries all before it except, unfortunately, either adequate definition of what it means, or – except at a very micro-level – any practical solutions to the problems which it seeks to define.

I shall argue below that an understanding of the history of human use of resources could have helped escape this impasse, had either developmentalists or environmentalists seriously sought illumination from the past. The fact that sustainability should appear as a new idea is a product of the ignorant a-historicism of most modern social and environmental science. There has been an extraordinary period during which it has, for the first time in human history, come to be thought that the 'second world within the world of nature' [*Glacken, 1963*] was all that mattered, with ability wholly to master its living and non-living environment. The rather sudden awakening to recognition that 'mastery over nature' has entailed no sort of mastery over natural process has not yet led to widespread acceptance that lessons can be learned from a long human past. Before we come to this, however, some obscurities of modern thinking about sustainability need first to be analysed if we are to see the relevance of historical experience.

THE SEARCH FOR CLARIFICATION

Problems with an Operational Definition

To write of 'development that meets the goals of the present without compromising the ability of future generations to meet their own needs' [*World Commission, 1987: 43*] is more to offer a statement of intent than provide a workable definition. Much the same can be said of the World Conservation Strategy's ecologically oriented emphasis on 'management of human use of the biosphere so that it may yield the greatest sustainable benefit to present generations while maintaining its potential to meet the needs and aspirations of future generations' [*IUCN, 1980, 1: 1*]. Redclift's [*1987*] whole book seeks a definition in terms of political economy, but fails to offer one, though Simon [*1989*] argues that only such a political-economy perspective can achieve enlightenment. In a prize-winning essay, Barbier [*1987: 103*] stresses the impossibility of analysing economic, social, cultural and ecological transformations separately from one another, while the quantitative dimension, 'associated with increases in the material means available to those . . . in poverty', and the qualitative dimension of 'ensuring the long-term ecological, social, and cultural, potential for supporting economic activity and structural change' are 'mutually reinforcing and inseparable'. Though true, this does not really provide clarification. There are several other attempts in the literature to deal with these multi-dimensional obscurities and they take us little further, perhaps because a confusion of relative and absolute scarcities is involved, as Underwood and King [*1989*] suggest in another context.

The Contribution of 'Steady-statism'

Paradoxically, the elitist and unrealistic 'steady-statists' provide a sharper cutting edge through the maze, though one used better by a different school of environmental economists than by themselves. The 'steady-state' school was created in its modern form by Georgescu-Roegen [*1971*], though he later introduced some important caveats [e.g. *Georgescu-Roegen, 1979*]. Focus on the flow of energy obtained from the natural environment, through the economic system, calls attention to the physical laws of thermodynamics and conservation and hence to entropy. Logically, this seems to demand constraint on the throughputs of energy and matter, to levels sustainable in terms of resource availability and the assimilative capacity of the biosphere. In Daly's [1984: 29] analogy of a boat in which increasing weight, however well-distributed through Pareto optimality, will ultimately sink the boat, what is missing from the operation of the market economy is 'an independent limit on the scale of the economic subsystem'. The question becomes one of determining that limit, and then devising policy levers to ensure that it is not exceeded.

The steady-statists' argument has many flaws, ably summed up by Perrings [1987: 141–52]. Their position gives them little room for manoeuvre, and they tend to repeat themselves, but sometimes with useful insight. Daly [1988: 49–53] was elaborating his earlier ideas [Daly, 1973; 1977; 1980] in suggesting that aggregated national accounts should include three elements: accumulation of capital in 'stocks' that get used up and 'funds' which wear out, the service yielded by these accumulations, and the entropic throughput of matter and energy out of which stocks and funds are replaced and maintained. Therefore a conservationally and socially appropriate economic behaviour would not maximise accumulation but seek only satisfying levels, while minimising throughput and maximising benefits. By reference back to Hicks' [1948] insistence that the measure of income should be what people can consume without impoverishing themselves, Daly and Cobb [1989: 70–71] later developed this argument to suggest that income obtained by resource depletion, as of the forests of a developing country, is in truth not a measurement of growth at all, but of economic decline. There are many non steady-statists who might agree.

A Way Out of the Dilemma

There is some similarity to at least the 'steady-statism' of an open system, importing and exporting both matter and energy, in the recent emphasis of Pearce et al. [1990: 1–22] on maintaining stocks of natural capital. This is argued in a more practical context which aims to set out the conditions of choice in a developmental situation. Elsewhere, Pearce and Turner [1990: 24] define sustainability by saying that: 'it involves maximising the net benefits of economic development, subject to maintaining the services and quality of natural resources over time'. They go on to stress that 'maintenance' involves the utilisation of renewable resources at a rate not more than equal to the natural rate of regeneration or reproduction, and optimising the efficient use and substitutability of non-renewable resources. This goes only some way toward escaping the 'steady-state' trap. However, whereas Daly and Cobb [1989: 71] would describe any reduction of non-renewable resources as unsustainable, the Pearce and

Turner definition compares with what Turner [*1988: 6*] calls the 'sustainable growth mode' and O'Riordan [*1988: 30*] 'sustainable utilisation'; both are in contradistinction to pure sustainability which would allow only for redistribution within a homeostatic, no-growth steady-state economy. The essence of sustainable growth is seen in the application of conservation rules to maintain the regenerative capacity of renewable resources, to guide technological change so as to switch from non-renewable to renewable resources wherever physically possible, and to develop a phasing policy for the necessary use of non-renewable resources.

O'Riordan [*1988: 30*] however adds, almost as an aside, the possibility that 'inherent rates of renewability can be enhanced through scientific management'. This is also allowed for by Pearce *et al.* [*1989: 44*] in calling for maintenance through time of the value of all capital stocks, man made and natural, compensating for reduction by new investments. More explicitly, Pearce *et al.* [*1990: 15*] write of 'natural capital augmentation'. It seems a tortuous route from the laws of entropy to recognition that while there is indeed a set of natural limitations, there might also be a sustainable way out. Yet this seemingly small rider transforms the entire argument, and makes it possible to move forward toward a realistic, scale-free, definition of what sustainable development means, and how it might be achieved.

THE NATURE OF RENEWABILITY AND SUBSTITUTABILITY

The Necessity of Change

From this point forward I adopt a more positive view, not of the present realities of excessive resource exploitation, but of the possibilities of sustainable growth or utilisation as defined above. There is, indeed, little point in seeking a research agenda if such a more positive view is not adopted, and some if its parameters need to be firmly stated. A strictly conservationist position is not practicable, for it is impossible to use even a renewable natural resource and at the same time leave it unaltered, with exactly the same qualities as before. Nor can human needs be satisfied without some consumption of non-renewables. Even if it is irreversible, alteration is not necessarily degradation, which has the meaning of reduction to a lower rank, and is therefore a concept based on human perception [*Blaikie and Brookfield, 1987: 1*]. It does no violence to sustainability to point out that conversion of a forest into well-managed agricultural land is not degradation if the product from the new use is of greater total utility to people, and can be maintained through time.

Furthermore, natural resources do not remain in unaltered condition even when unused. Erosion and deposition are natural processes, soils become leached of their nutrients, trees age and die, initially oliogotrophic lakes become eutrophic naturally. The creation of entropy is a basic condition of nature, not only of human use. But at the same time forests are renewed, new soil is formed, hybridisation creates new variants of life forms, plant invasions and the creation of new vegetation complexes are continual, especially in response to the climatic change that has been a reality over the whole period of human occupation of the earth. All these processes, degrading, restoring and replacing, operate at very different rates both intrinsically, and under varied site conditions.

Change is a natural condition, and change at the hand of human beings is inevitable. 'A nonequilibrium closed system [with or without human interference] inevitably moves from a sequence of past known states to a different sequence of future unknown states' [*Perrings, 1987: 150*]. These considerations are destructive to the 'absolute scarcity' notions on which so much of steady-state economics relies. Still more are they damaging to the underlying logic of 'deep ecology ecocentrism' [*O'Riordan, 1981; O'Riordan and Turner, 1983*]. The role of human activity in relation to nature is to modify ecosystems and accelerate change in natural systems, while at the same time further opening systems by introducing new elements and shifting others from place to place.

Alternatives to Reliance on Natural Regeneration

Reliance on natural regenerative processes is more than an ideal; it is also technically much the cheapest way of attaining sustainability. However, the cost of reliance on natural reproduction is the cost of not using the resource, such as fish, or a forest, at a higher rate than can permit replacement, or polluting a river at no higher a rate than is capable of being purified by bio-degradation; or leaving the resource totally unused after 'harvest' until such time as natural reproduction has taken place. There is a more expensive alternative which, in these examples, is to invest in aquaculture, or reforestation, or construct complex plant for water purification and waste-recycling. Natural reproduction can be availed only at very low rates of utilisation except in the most naturally productive or resilient ecosystems. A low-intensity shifting cultivation regime permits restoration of land capability – if not the original forest – if time is allowed [*Nye and Greenland, 1960*]. Much higher rates of utilisation can be sustained in the wetlands that, for this reason, were perhaps the first sites of dense human habitation [*Sherratt, 1980*]. However, any increase of intensity above naturally supportable rates always and everywhere demands a considerable input of human artifice.

Wilkinson's 'Ecological Model of Development'

This has been so from the beginning, and it is implicit in the whole theory of agricultural intensification [*Boserup, 1965; 1981; Brookfield, 1972; 1984; 1986*], and indeed in almost any shift away from the pre-capitalist peasant 'steady-statism' of Chayanov [*1966*]. In a more developmental context, Wilkinson's [*1973*] 'ecological model of development' might have provided the basis of an interpretative theory of sustainable development had it been taken up. His work was in fact almost disregarded until rescued from obscurity by Common [*1988*]. Wilkinson took inspiration from Boserup [*1965*] by arguing that technical progress arose from resource scarcity. He contrasted an idealised pre-capitalist situation, based largely on the generalisations of Wynne-Edwards [*1962*] and other writers, in which 'natural populations . . . build up a pattern and a rate of resource use which the environment can sustain indefinitely' [*Wilkinson, 1973: 21*], with development as a 'process of solving a succession of problems which from time to time threaten the productive system and the sufficiency of our subsistence. In effect, human societies out of ecological equilibrium have to run to keep up; their development does not necessarily imply any longterm improvement in the quality of human life' [*ibid.: 105*].

    Wilkinson was perhaps over-simplifying in attributing the whole of human technical progress to inventiveness in the face of resource scarcity, beginning his own detailed argument with the need to overcome shortages of wood in seventeenth- and eighteenth-century Britain. None the less, I am wholly with him in regarding human ability in adaptation as the key to what has been sustainable in development throughout history, calling today for research and development effort 'directed towards improving ways of exploiting lasting resources', so as to make humankind the 'master of change', rather than the master of nature [*Wilkinson, 1973: 216–18*].

THE IMPORTANCE OF HUMAN ARTIFICE IN RESOURCE MANAGEMENT

Continual Adaptation

There is therefore an insufficiently examined midway path between the rigid natural determinism of the 'limits to growth' [*Meadows et al., 1972; Barney, 1980*] and steady-state schools, on the one hand, and 'technological cornucopianism' such as that of Beckermann [*1972*], Simon and Kahn, (eds.) [*1984*] or Singer [*1987*], or even the more cautious formulation of Smil [*1987*]. It lies, as Common [*1988: 34*] paraphrases Wilkinson, in the view that the essential quality of historically sustained development is continual adaptation. There is an alternative path between total reliance on natural renewability and wanton resource destruction, and the mediating force is successful human adaptive artifice.

This latter is a quality. It lies in between quantifiable land, labour and capital; it is not captured by 'entrepreneurship' or even by 'technology', though both these are essential elements. Thus the long-lived replacement of shifting cultivation by crop/fallow rotation was successful human artifice of which the most important condition was not technology, but reorganisation of land tenure and labour. Stinting the use of common property resources has the similar effect of converting unsustainability into sustainability, and its condition is codification of common-sense rules, and their enforcement [*McCay and Acheson (eds.), 1987; Perrings, 1987*]. Initially, the replacement of scarce wood by abundant coal required no new technology beyond adaptation of ancient mining methods developed for other purposes; whatever its long-term effects, its immediate consequence was to take unsustainable pressure off the woodlands and hence help conserve the soil. It was substitution of an abundant non-renewable for a scarce renewable resource of a type still under heavy pressure in many parts of the world.

Natural and Human Forces in Opposition and Conjunction

Blaikie and Brookfield [*1987*] were writing of the degradation of renewable resources rather than sustainability, but our reasoning has relevance to the present argument. We were seeking to bring together researched historical experience, physical explanation of degradation, and a meaningful political economy of the conditions of resource management. We suggested [*ibid.: 9*] that net land degradation can be summed up as the product of an equation, in which the effects of human interference added to natural degrading processes are offset to greater or lesser degree by natural reproduction plus restorative human management. We sought to emphasise that some human artifice has the effect, purposive or otherwise, of conserving a resource, and that in the constant experimentation that underlies all development not everything is destructive. Some creations of landesque capital through human artifice, for example the terracing of mountainsides which would otherwise slide away, have endured many hundreds of years.

A SOCIAL DEFINITION OF ENVIRONMENTAL SUSTAINABILITY

Sustainability and Unsustainability in Historical Perspective

The progressive substitution of one resource for another, progressive improvements through artifice and technology in the ways in which both renewable and non-renewable resources are managed, improvements in efficiency in the use of energy and the conversion of resources into useful products, and organisational adaptations which improve the return to land, labour and capital, are therefore not new ideas. They are historical facts, and the means by which all sustainable development has been achieved. They have assisted the natural reproduction of resource capability, or negentropy. They have certainly not in all cases succeeded in preventing resource destruction, and much less so in preventing pollution from wastes, until quite lately only a localised problem that was rarely perceived as very serious. But they have achieved a great deal.

The new situation created in our present time is primarily quantitative in nature, in that the rate of impact on resources and the environment has accelerated exponentially through population growth, major increases in per capita consumption, and the global quest for rapid development. The rate at which non-renewables are being consumed is a matter of concern to all who do not believe in infinite substitutability, and the rate at which renewables are being reduced and damaged, sometimes irreversibly over foreseeable time, exceeds that of any previous historical period.

However, a further difference between present and past also lies in the fact that the social pressures on the resource manager, of whatever scale, have become qualitatively different. Through the pervasive impact of a commercial economy, decision-making is no longer localised, and a multitude of decisions with impact on resources is taken in total or partial ignorance of that impact, or in spite of knowledge that damage – somewhere – is severe. Substitutability in a global market has come to mean that a whole region can be degraded if there are other regions on which to draw, a process which Pearce *et al.* [*1989: 45–7*] term 'importing and exporting sustainability'. The degree of security in which on-the-spot resource management decisions are taken has been gravely eroded, a basic argument of Blaikie and Brookfield [*1987*]. As Barbier [*1987*] correctly noted, the quantitative and qualitative aspects neither of the damage nor of the remedy can be separated. They must therefore be brought together.

A First Interim Conclusion

Perhaps we can therefore adapt Pearce and Turner [*1990: 24*]. We can agree that sustainable development, or growth, involves maximising and optimally distributing the net benefits of economic development. We can also agree that the services and qualities of natural resources must at the same time be maintained – and also restored or improved – into the foreseeable future. However, we need to add the condition that these must be achieved while re-establishing and reaffirming the conditions of security under which resource managers operate.

This is not 'steady state', nor is it unbridled growth; nor is it an appeal to the market principle on the lines of Coase [*1960/1977*] or any of his numerous successors, a topic on which a critical but constructive analysis of contemporary thinking was recently provided by Pezzey [*1988*]. On the contrary it calls for new institutional approaches to development, and presents a huge challenge to development research and practice in order to make it work. It does, however, allow us a realistic research agenda.

THE COSTS OF SUSTAINABLE MANAGEMENT

A Problem of Measurement

The most urgent problem for research is therefore to investigate what is needed in order to develop management strategies, technology and artifice that will ensure us of sustainable growth as far forward as it is possible to project present conditions and trends. It is simplest to do this in the context of agriculture, where much is already known. Sustainable agriculture, though said in some quarters to have originated only in the period before the Second World War [e.g. *Lockeretz, 1988*], is as old as agriculture itself. Most of the modern 'sustainable' technologies such as organic farming, minimum tillage, erosion control, crop diversity, tightening of nutrient cycles, efficient irrigation, maintenance of cover, agro-forestry and effective rotations, can be identified both in ancient farming systems throughout the world, and in present farming systems still practised in areas unaffected by the modern wave of chemicalisation and mechanisation. A handbook of the new methods, such as that of Unger and McCalla [*1980*], can usefully be read alongside a comprehensive statement of tropical farming systems such as that of Ruthenberg [*1980*], to cite only two examples where comparison could be informative. However, whereas some of these systems have advantages of cost reduction per crop due to reduction of inputs, many conservationist methods seek directly to sustain productivity over from two or three to very many years. This they do by the creation of landesque capital in the form of terraces, dams, contour-based systems, drainage, and the reorganisation of farms. These imply saving.

Notwithstanding a prevailing view that farmers 'will not invest in sustainable technologies for which the profits cannot be immediately captured' [*Altieri et al., 1984: 186*], there is abundant empirical evidence that they will, and do so with or without subsidy, if an ultimate benefit can be perceived. There are many forms of land use which operate on a longer-term benefit horizon. This is an important issue for sustainability as a whole, far beyond agriculture, for enhancement of natural regeneration on the land, in the waters and in the air, require both constraint in harvesting and waste creation, and investment for the future. They have costs that cannot be measured by price signals within the short time frame of the market economy. Writing of sustainable development, a working group which I chaired added that: 'To improve both the quality of human life, and the qualities of the natural environment on which that life is based is not impossible: it has been done in the past, and is being done in places today. It requires, however, substantial savings from consumption in order to provide investment for the future' [IFIAS-ISSC-UNU, 1989: 28].

The Larger Cost of Doing Nothing

The cost of adopting none of these methods will, in the long term, be much higher. A striking, if extreme, illustration comes from society's present demands on tropical hardwood timber resources, without significant deliberate replacement, far exceeding any rate which would ensure a continuing resource for future generations. Similarly, we are drawing continuously on the resources of the soil, and it has, for example, been estimated that if top-soil losses from the corn belt of the United States continue at current rates, crop yields might be cut by 15–30 per cent by 2030 [Korsching and Nowak, 1982]. There are many examples, both historical and contemporary, that can be used to demonstrate these costs. Perhaps the most extreme of them come from the former bloc of Socialist countries. For example, the multi-faceted Aral Sea crisis looks like becoming a classic case of the unwanted side effects of ambitious development in a sensitive environment, with 'repair' costs conservatively estimated at 30 billion roubles [N.F. Glazovsky, personal communication.]. From China, Hoppe [1987: 69] quotes Chen Hua in writing that: 'Some of these comrades tell me that here [in the state farms on the Northern fringe of the Tarim Basin] also they have the problem of the "Four Modernizations". These are salinisation, desertification, soil deterioration, and gullying. Soil deterioration means that the land is planted for three years in succession, but after that, the fertility and, correspondingly, the productivity also decline.'

Estimating Costs Payable for a 'Free Good'

Many safer management strategies are known to reduce both natural and induced damage and to aid, accelerate or improve on natural reproduction, but they are costly. Many are labour-intensive, and hence in opposition to present public and private goals for social and economic development. Many require capital investment, whether in industry or in agriculture and forestry, and much of this is investment in detail, and hence at the cost of a multitude of individual producers. Many have a cost in foregone production and consumption, at least in the short term, and this cost can be large; it is not readily borne by the very poor. However, at least some of the very poor do meet these costs, where the alternative is total loss of livelihood [e.g. *Johnson et al., 1982; Lipton, 1989*]. Almost all such strategies add to the cost of production, and hence price, and not many yield a short-term return in improved production that is commensurate with the cost.

In broad terms, costs payable to the environment in order to continue to exist with a usable set of qualities are capable of at least estimation, even quantification. A striking example from the United States is provided by valuation of the farm capital works created under soil conservation programmes initiated in the 1930s, by Pavelis [*1983*]. Standardised to 1977 dollars and amortised, the value of these investments peaked in 1955 at a level equal to 4.8 per cent of the net land value, then declined to reach 3.7 per cent by 1980. Pavelis argues that the decline represents consumption of capital for production purposes, in consequence of a 'production pressure on resources'. Modern development has hitherto tended very seriously to draw on and reduce the reproductive capacity both of renewable resources and of human improvements made in an earlier period. Hoppe [*1987: 76*] has argued that:

> Reproduction exists everywhere . . . under the impact of development and capital accumulation it is used, drained, and finally dried up. It can only regain its place, if the specific impetus of 'development' and capital accumulation is rejected. The reproduction paradigm may lead to a better understanding of what growth for a society and its environment means, and how difficult it is to obtain, if our guardianship of the globe is taken seriously.

A Second Interim Conclusion

Taken together, the work of Pavelis and the reasoning of Hoppe lead toward a second interim conclusion. To make development sustainable it is necessary both that natural reproduction of capabilities be not drawn down, and that investment in conserving or improving capabilities be undertaken and sustained. Only by meeting these costs can the environment of future generations become a productive and wholesome artefact, built of human artifice allied to and enhancing natural reproduction. Given the pressing need to put figures on what we mean by 'sustainable development' it would seem to be a task of high priority to use available knowledge so that we may begin to have some idea of what is involved. Moreover, the cost of not meeting the costs of sustainability is impossibly high, if a long view is taken. We cannot continue to have development on the cheap.

This conclusion has implications for the method of costing, and in particular for the use of cost/benefit analysis which is such anathema to so many environmentalists, believing as they do that positive discount rates encourage exploitation rather than conservation in almost any circumstances. This is a technical aspect on which constructive discussion is recently offered by Pearce *et al.* [*1990: 23–66*]. Whether or not cost/benefit analysis can be modified to incorporate sustainability, it is clear that it has very large problems in dealing with risk and uncertainty. Yet these are essential elements in any agenda of development research, whether geared toward sustainability or otherwise. This whole large issue must now command our attention.

SUSTAINABILITY WITHIN UNCERTAINTY

The First Set of Uncertainties

The task of prescribing for sustainability would be simpler if the needs of even the next generation could be predicted with accuracy. It would be simpler also if we could hold technology constant, or alternatively assume with security such improvements as a determinable increase in crop yields due to breeding advances. It would be simpler if we really even knew the rates at which tropical forest trees grow. In fact none of this is certain, and any attempt to operationalise sustainability must of necessity involve a large element of guesswork. Moreover, in dealing with sustainable futures it is important to decide on how far we can or should project trends which depend on the large chemical inputs of modern agriculture, themselves the cause of a major set of environmental problems.

The Fallaciousness of 'Carrying Capacity'

The problems can be exemplified from the frequent use of the concept of 'carrying capacity' [e.g. *Pearce and Turner, 1990: 241ff; Daly and Cobb, 1989: 369–70*], being the maximum stock of animals which an ecosystem or region can carry without loss of ability to regenerate, or even provide support. Over many years, this concept – which generally ignores environmental variability through time – has also been applied to human populations. Pearce [*1988*] uses human carrying capacity, albeit guardedly, as a proxy measure of natural resource degradation, presumably having missed the critique by Blaikie and Brookfield [*1987: 28–34*]. Sometimes, this concept is used in relation to high-input systems of production. In this way an optimistic pan-tropical study of carrying capacity to the year 2000 [*FAO, 1982; Higgins et al., 1984*] obtained a mainly good result, even for most of Africa, on the dubious assumption that green revolution technology can everywhere be applied. Presumably, a calculation employing present technology and its product would yield results too dismal for an international organisation to print. Yet on such a basis Allan [*1965*] found large parts of Africa to be already overpopulated in relation to carrying capacity a generation ago. Allan also drew attention to the historical fact of major decline in the quality of agricultural technology, due to the interfering effects of colonialism and all its consequences on the old indigenous production systems. Using the latter, yet a third set of conclusions might be drawn. What is the proper basis to use if we are to begin to prescribe a sustainable path for African agricultural development?

The unreality of the human carrying capacity model demonstrates the difficulty of relating resources to future needs and future ability to meet them. At a global scale, Smil [*1987*] points to a large reserve of potential arable land created by the energy-inefficient use of so much cultivable land for range-fed livestock; if we admit the possibility of change in the composition of diets, future land needs are changed. If we assume future animals all to be stall-fed, they are changed again, and if we make projections as to what bio-technology may yield, they are of still another order. Yet it is equally unreal to calculate future needs on the basis only of contemporary agro-technology and practice, as the fate of several dozen predictions that global famine would have struck us before now, made since the early 1950s, clearly demonstrates.

Environmental Goals and Production Goals

Sustainable development research cannot begin from ideals derived from some non-existent past. It is necessary to begin by accepting the innovation that has taken place, however harmful some of it has been, and seek amelioration by putting 'environmental concerns at the center and then work out a production plan' which will meet both environmental and production goals, as Parikh [*1988: 376*] suggests. This is not to say that the production goals should be retained unaltered, or that some should not simply be abandoned. However, in very many cases, as several essays in Parikh's collection show, greater efficiency of resource use, reduced environmental damage and pollution, and even a path toward sustainability can be devised through appropriate research and its application. Ghatak [*1988*] argues cogently that both for environmental reasons, and also because of diminishing returns from the seed-fertiliser green revolution, any new 'green revolution' for a sustainable future must depend on biotechnology, integrated pest management and biological control rather than chemical plant protection. Nor can such research be purely technical, for there are huge social problems associated with any such set of changes, that need to be resolved. There is further reason to research along this path, for there seems to be a good probability that a biologically based and more diversified post-modern agriculture might be less vulnerable to natural variability and resulting damage than what has gone before. This is of particular importance in view of the great new uncertainties that cannot be ignored.

The Oft-disregarded Problem of Environmental Uncertainty

It would always be much simpler to prescribe for a sustainable future if the environment behaved according to the mean values used to describe such of its properties as rainfall and temperature, and processes such as erosion and transportation rates. Instead, drought, storm, flood and unseasonable temperature are the common episodic condition of most parts of the planet. It is a familiar experience that a development project which appears entirely sustainable under favourable conditions is shown to be completely unsustainable when confronted by untoward natural events, entirely predictable in every respect but the timing of their occurrence. Porter *et al.* [*1991*] show how yields notionally calculated forward on the basis of mean rainfall conditions for an unsuccessful resettlement project in Kenya would, when projected backward over the experienced rainfall of a 21-year period, have been achieved in only three of these years. Re-calculation of the project cost/benefit analysis on this latter basis, also removing other dubious assumptions, converted a strongly positive into a negative internal rate of return. Most of this could have been foreseen. This is an extreme but not at all remarkable case. A much greater example of misguided optimism is that of the southern Great Plains of the United States, settled and farmed in a favourable period, then smitten simultaneously and disastrously by the coincidence of economic depression and a series of hot, dry years in the 1930s. Events of this nature, of which the most catastrophic have been the succession of Sahelian droughts since 1972, can have a devastating effect on designs for 'sustainable development'.

A Third Interim Conclusion

If we are to be realistic, the definition and practice of 'sustainable development' must be therefore undertaken in this context of environmental uncertainty. Moreover, wholly new elements of uncertainty are now presented to us in well-argued terms in consequence of the major scientific developments of the 1980s. The still-new information concerning global climatic uncertainty has to be overlain onto all previous discussion of the environmental consequences of human activity. The development debate, before it has seriously begun to take on board the costs of environmental interference as an integral dimension of total welfare, has already to face uncertainty in what has until very lately been regarded as given and secure: the basic natural environment of all human activity. The speed at which environmental change has become a major issue is exceeded only by the speed of the remarkable political transformations of the past year; both create uncertainty, and uncertainty is the environment of this conference. I have until this point ignored climatic uncertainty since it has no significant place in the sustainability literature with the signal exception of the contributions of Conway [*1985; 1987*] on climatic shocks and stresses, which have somehow achieved notice, especially in the recent writings of Pearce and his colleagues, where other warnings have not.

'Global Climatic Change' and Other Uncertainties

This is not the place in which to go into a lengthy discussion of the question of global climatic change. Suffice to say that if the reality approaches median or above predictions of temperature increase during the coming century, the rate of increase may exceed the capacity of many plant species to adapt, leading to devastating biological changes that will overwhelm any possible but selective benefit from an atmosphere richer in carbon dioxide. It follows that all and any measures to contain and reduce emissions of greenhouse gases, in developing and developed countries alike, are a necessary condition for a sustainable global future without enormous dislocation.

There are also other considerations. Since the early 1970s there has been something of a cluster of the major disturbances to global atmospheric circulation popularly described as El Niño episodes, and their equally dislocating converse. This is not necessarily related to 'global climatic change' for there was another such cluster from the 1870s to 1918. Severe El Niño events produce serious droughts throughout a large part of the tropics and sub-tropics, and major anomalies elsewhere. Sometimes, as in 1988, there are intervening events when pressure anomalies are opposite to those of El Niño years, and these can produce extremely heavy rainfall and serious flooding in the same regions. The probability within which contingency planning must rationally operate is that a period of strong anomalies in world weather may continue over at least the short-term future. There are also well-established regional trends of long duration in rainfall, involving in the Sudan, for example, a 20 per cent decline in rainfall resources over the span of a single generation since mid-century [*Hulme, 1990*]. We live in a period of climatic uncertainty, compounded by the still-unclear consequences of human interference in the composition of the atmosphere. It would be folly, and wilful blindness to increasingly well-founded scientific advance warning, not to take the possible eventualities for the boundary conditions of development into account.

These considerations must, of necessity, be incorporated into development research which seeks sustainable solutions. Drought, flood and famine, already characteristic of the past two decades, must be thought of as part of the probable environment within which present unsustainability must be phased out, and new solutions designed. No circular 'steady state' can apply in such conditions, and it seems very likely that 'natural capital augmentation' will become the only route to sustainability, as Pearce *et al.* [*1990: 15*] argue in a more general context. Better resource management, greater diversity, and far greater protection against degradation, are the best insurance. Certainly, the human inventiveness and adaptability which I have sought to stress as basic to both past and future sustainability will be more than ever required.

CONCLUSION

Scaling Down and Scaling Up the Issues

Research toward sustainable strategies must embrace all scales from global to the local scale at which most development practice operates. If we are to do this in such a way as to achieve co-operation at both national and local levels in the Third World we must do so in a positive, forward looking way, and not by appealing only to the conservationist ethic. This latter is not unattractive to some people in developing countries, but to a great many others it makes ecology seem 'distant water that would not quench present thirst' [*Glaeser and Steidl-Meier, 1987: 152*]. On the other hand a set of programmes that offers a sustainable and productive future, with reduction in the environmental damage that is presently very obvious to very many, could have strong appeal.

Helpfully, Lowrance *et al.* [*1986*], following Douglass [*1984*], offer a hierarchical approach to the study of sustainable agriculture that is capable of wider generalisation. They distinguish 'agronomic sustainability' at the level of the field, where the objective is sustained yield. This fits into 'microeconomic' sustainability at the level of the farm, where it is possible to shift inputs between different fields. In turn, this nests into 'ecological sustainability' at the level of a whole agricultural landscape, where the objective is maintenance of life-support capacity over longer time scales. Finally, it is necessary for the success of any sustainable strategy to aim for 'macroeconomic' sustainability which determines the conditions of production. This approach, shifting attention recursively

between management of a specific resource, the local and larger organisational and regional systems where management takes place, and the
state, would seem to offer a structure within which research for sustainable
development might productively be organised. In such a frame, the political
economy and social elements that I have treated only lightly in this article
could most readily be combined with sustainable management of the natural
and made environment.

Introducing an Appropriate Political Economy

Such might be a political economy that, as Perrings [*1987: 160–167*]
cogently argues, should embrace both a principle of common property,
within which inter-generational equity and institutional flexibility against
uncertainty can most effectively be managed, and also a principle of private
accountability which departs some considerable way from the free market
solution. Perrings argues [*ibid.: 164*] that wherever there is a time or distance
delay in the transmission of external effects of any action, it will never be
socially optimal to leave decision and the settlement of resulting dispute
in private hands. Following Solow [*1971*], he advocates an 'environmental
bond' set at the estimated cost of the worst-case outcome, refundable in
whole or part if appropriate investments or other adaptations are taken
to prevent this outcome. It could be added that it might be refunded
with a bonus if the quality of the environment and its resilience to shocks
are enhanced. In such a way, the costing of repairing, maintaining and
improving the qualities of the environment which this paper advocates as
a major research task, could have very practical social value. It requires,
however, a strong civil society that would understand and support such
measures, at all levels from the local to the international.

Not only does this not exist today, except among some local communities,
but the chances of its achievement are perhaps lower than at any previous
time during the long slide of faith in the institutions of interventionism that
has been in progress since their peak in the 1930s and 1940s. An alarming
paradox underlines the link between recent political events in Europe and
Asia, and the urgent problem of making development more sustainable.
There is serious risk that the baby of social priorities in development may be
thrown out in the extremely dirty bathwater of corrupt and inefficient central
economic command. At the same time, we are faced with incontrovertible
evidence that the major social priority of sound environmental management
has been disastrously neglected in east and west, north and south alike.
There has been general failure of governments and their advisers alike to
recognise that the environment is the most important of all social goods. The
ultimate contradiction in all societies everywhere, that between individual
benefit and social benefit, cannot be captured by the market economy, nor

it seems by any interventionist polity that this century has known.

The Need to Inform

My final conclusion is simply reached. Undoing unsustainability and building sustainability in its place will be an enormous task, against great opposition, and made much worse by uncertainties, aggravated by human action, with which we have to live in the foreseeable future. It is further made worse by the widespread distrust of government. We need to pay attention to the past and to the immense fund of knowledge possessed by resource managers on the ground, but in saying this I do not go all the way with the populists such as Chambers [*1984*] and Richards [*1985*], or even with the World Conservation Strategy [*IUCN, 1980*]. The political economy within which resource management takes place is of fundamental importance, and if that continues to be based on licence to exploitation and greed, nothing will improve. Reforms at the level of the state and society are a *sine qua non* of sustainable development, and a significant measure of intervention cannot be avoided.

However, willingness by governments to put social priorities, including the central social priority of the environment, ahead of other priorities, demands the support of a global public not beguiled and befuddled by either cornucopianism or misguided ecological idealism, but informed about what is necessary and what is possible, and what it will cost in financial terms, in institutional terms, and in terms of shared social responsibility, to achieve a sustainable future. This is an interdisciplinary task, and one that calls for a wider definition of development studies and research than has hitherto been the practice. Yet provision of this information, essential to any social action, is our agenda.

REFERENCES

Allan, W., 1965, *The African Husbandman*, Edinburgh: Oliver & Boyd.
Altieri, M.A., Letourneau, D.K. and J.R. Davis, 1984, 'The Requirements of Sustainable Agroecosystems', in G.K. Douglass (ed.), *Agricultural Sustainability in a Changing World Order*, Boulder, CO: Westview Press, pp.175–89.
Apthorpe, R. and A. Krahl, 1986, *Development Studies: Critique and Renewal*, Leiden: E.J. Brill.
Barbier, E.B., 1987, 'The Concept of Sustainable Development', *Environmental Conservation*, Vol.14, No.2, pp.101–10.
Barnett, H.J. and C. Morse, 1963, *Scarcity and Growth: the Economics of Natural Resource Scarcity*, Baltimore, MD: Johns Hopkins Press.
Barney, G.O., 1980, *The Global 2000 Report to the President [of the United States]: Entering the Twenty-first Century* (2 vols.), Oxford: Pergamon Press.
Baumol, W.J. and W.E. Oates, 1979, *Economics, Environmental Policy, and the Quality of Life*, Englewood Cliffs, NJ: Prentice-Hall.

Beckermann, W., 1972, 'Economists, Scientists, and Environmental Catastrophe', *Oxford Economic Papers*, Vol.24, No.3, pp.327–44.

Blaikie, P. and H. Brookfield, with contributions by others, 1987, *Land Degradation and Society*, London and New York: Methuen.

Bohm, P. and A.V. Kneese (eds.), 1971, *The Economics of Environment*, London: Macmillan.

Boserup, E., 1965, *The Conditions of Agricultural Growth: The Economics of Agrarian Change under Population Pressure*, Chicago, IL: Aldine.

Boserup, E., 1981, *Population and Technology*, Oxford: Blackwell.

Boulding, K.E., 1966, 'The Economics of the Coming Spaceship Earth', in H. Jarrett (ed.), *Environmental Quality in a Growing Economy*, Baltimore, MD Johns Hopkins University Press, pp.3–14.

Brookfield, H.C., 1972, 'Intensification and Disintensification in Pacific Agriculture: A Theoretical Approach', *Pacific Viewpoint*, Vol.13, No.1, pp.30–48.

Brookfield, H. C., 1975, *Interdependent Development*, London: Methuen.

Brookfield, H.C., 1984, 'Intensification Revisited', *Pacific Viewpoint*, Vol.25, No.1, pp.15–44.

Brookfield, H.C., 1986, 'Intensification Intensified: Prehistoric Intensive Agriculture in the Tropics' (review article), *Archaeology in Oceania*, Vol.21, No.3, pp.177–80.

Brookfield, H.C., 1988, 'Sustainable Development and the Environment' (review article), *Journal of Development Studies*, Vol.25, No.1, pp.126–35.

Chambers, R., 1984, *Rural Development: Putting the Last First*, London: Longman.

Chayanov, A.V., 1966, *The Theory of Peasant Economy*, edited by D. Thorner, B. Kerblay and R.E.F. Smith, and translated from originals in German (1923) and Russian (1925), Homewood, IL: Richard D. Irwin for the American Economic Association.

Coase, R.H., 1960, 'The Problem of Social Costs', *Journal of Law and Economics*, Vol.3, pp.1–44. Reprinted 1977 in R. Dorfman and N. Dorfman (eds.), *Economics of the Environment* (second edition), New York: Norton, pp.142–71.

Common, M., 1988, '"Poverty and Progress" Revisited', in D. Collard, D. Pearce and D. Ulph (eds.), *Economics, Growth and Sustainable Environments: Essays in Memory of Richard Lecomber*, London: Macmillan, pp.14–39.

Conway, G., 1985, 'Agroecosystem Analysis', *Agricultural Administration*, Vol.20, No.1, pp.31–55.

Conway, G., 1987, 'The Properties of Agroecosystems', *Agricultural Systems*, Vol.24, No.2, pp.95–117.

Daly, H.E., 1973, 'Introduction to the Steady-state Economy', in H.E. Daly (ed.), *Toward a Steady-state Economy*, San Francisco, CA: W.H. Freeman, pp.1–31.

Daly, H.E., 1977, *Steady-state Economics*, San Francisco, CA: W.H. Freeman.

Daly, H.E., 1980, 'The Steady-state Economy: Toward a Political Economy of Biophysical Equilibrium and Moral Growth', in H.E. Daly (ed.), *Economics, Ecology, Ethics: Essays toward a Steady-state Economy*, San Francisco, CA: W.H. Freeman, pp.324–72.

Daly, H.E., 1984, 'Alternative Strategies for Integrating Economics and Ecology', in A.-M. Jansson (ed.), *Integration of Economy and Ecology–An Outlook for the Eighties*, Stockholm: University of Stockholm Press, pp.19–29.

Daly, H.E., 1988, 'On Sustainable Development and National Accounts', in D. Collard, D. Pearce and D. Ulph (eds.), *Economics, Growth and Sustainable Environments: Essays in Memory of Richard Lecomber*, London: Macmillan, pp.41–56.

Daly, H.E. and J.B. Cobb, 1989, *For the Common Good: Redirecting the Economy toward Community, the Environment and a Sustainable Future*, Boston, MA: Beacon Press.

Douglass, G.K., 1984, 'The Meanings of Agricultural Sustainability' in G.K. Douglass (ed.), *Agricultural Sustainability in a Changing World Order*, Boulder, CO: Westview Press, pp.3–29.

Engels, F., 1876/1970, 'The Part Played by Labour in the Transition from Ape to Man', [Written in 1876 and reprinted in translation] in K. Marx and F. Engels, *Selected Works* (3 vols.), Moscow: Progress Publishers, Vol.3, pp.66–77.

FAO, 1982, *Potential Population Supporting Capacities of Lands in the Developing World*, Technical Report on FAO/UNFPA Project INT 75/P13, Rome: Food and Agriculture

Organisation of the United Nations.

Fisher, A.C., 1981, *Resource and Environmental Economics*, New York: Cambridge University Press.

Georgescu-Roegen, N., 1971, *The Entropy Law and the Economic Process*, Cambridge, MA: Harvard University Press.

Georgescu-Roegen, N., 1979, 'Energy Analysis and Economic Evaluation', *Southern Economic Journal*, Vol.45, No.4, pp.1023–58.

Ghatak, S., 1988, 'Towards a Second Green Revolution: From Chemicals to New Biological Techniques in Agriculture in the Tropics for sustainable Development', in R. K. Turner (ed.), *Sustainable Environmental Management: Principles and Practice*, London: Bellhaven Press and Boulder, CO: Westview Press, pp.145–69.

Glacken, C.J., 1963, 'The Growing Second World Within the World of Nature', in F.R. Fosberg (ed.), *Man's Place in the Island Ecosystem*, Honolulu, HI: Bishop Museum Press, pp.75–100.

Glacken, C.J., 1967, *Traces on the Rhodian Shore: Nature and Culture in Western Thought from Ancient Times to the End of the Eighteenth Century*, Berkeley and Los Angeles, CA: University of California Press.

Glaeser, B. (ed.), 1984, *Ecodevelopment: Concepts, Projects, Strategies*, Oxford: Pergamon Press.

Glaeser, B. and P. Steidl-Meier, 1987, 'Rural Ecodevelopment Policy in China and the Origins of Economic Adjustment', in B. Glaeser (ed.), *Learning from China? Development and Environment in Third World Countries*, London: Allen & and Unwin, pp.144–61.

Hicks, J.R., 1948, *Value and Capital* (second edition), Oxford: Clarendon Press.

Higgins, G.M., A.M. Kassam and M. Shah, 1984, 'Land, Food and Population in the Developing World', *Nature and Resources*, Vol.20, No.3, pp.2–10.

Hoppe, T., 1987, 'An Essay on Reproduction: The Example of Xinjiang Uighur Autonomous Region', in B. Glaeser (ed.), *Learning from China? Development and Environment in Third World Countries*, London: Allen & Unwin, pp.56–84.

Hotelling, H., 1931, 'The Economics of Exhaustible Resources', *Journal of Political Economy*, Vol.39, No.2, pp.137–75. Reprinted, 1990, in A.C. Darnell (ed.), *The Collected Economics Articles of Harold Hotelling*, New York: Springer Verlag, pp.64–92.

Hulme, M., 1990, 'The changing rainfall resources of Sudan', *Transactions, Institute of British Geographers*, NS, Vol.15, No.1, pp.21–34.

IFIAS/ISSC/UNU, 1989, *The Human Dimensions of Global Change: An International Programme on Human Interactions with the Earth Report of the Tokyo International Symposium on the Human Response to Global Change, Tokyo, Japan, September 19–22, 1988*, Toronto: International Federation of Institutes of Advanced Studies, in co-operation with the International Social Science Council and the United Nations University.

IUCN, 1980, *World Conservation Strategy: Living Resource Conservation for Sustainable Development*, Gland, Switzerland: International Union for the Conservation of Nature and Resources, in co-operation with the United Nations Environment Programme and the World Wildlife Fund.

Johnson, K., Olson, E.A. and S. Manandhar, 1982, 'Environmental Knowledge and Response to Natural Hazards in Mountainous Nepal', *Mountain Research and Development*, Vol.2, No.2, pp.175–88.

Kemp, M.C., Long, N.V. and K. Shimomura, 1984, 'The Problem of Survival: A Closed Economy', in M.C. Kemp and N.V. Long (eds.), *Essays in the Economics of Exhaustible Resources*, Amsterdam: North Holland Publishers, pp.13–35.

Kneese, A.V., 1977, *Economics and the Environment*, New York: Penguin.

Korsching, P.F. and P.J. Nowak, 1982, 'Farmer Acceptance of Alternative Conservation Policies', *Agriculture and Environment*, Vol.7, No.1, pp.1–14.

Lecomber, J.R.C., 1975, *Economic Growth versus the Environment*, London: Macmillan.

Lipton, M., 1989, *New Strategies and Successful Examples for Sustainable Development in the Third World*, Testimony presented at a hearing on 'Sustainable Development and Economic Growth in the Third World', held by the Joint Economic Committee of the US

Congress, Subcommittee on Technology and National Security, 20 June 1989, Washington, DC: International Food Policy Institute.

Lockeretz, W., 1988, 'Open Questions in Sustainable Agriculture', *American Journal of Alternative Agriculture*, Vol.3, No.4, pp.174–81.

Lowrance, R., Hendrix, P.F. and E.P. Odum, 1986, 'A Hierarchical Approach to Sustainable Agriculture', *American Journal of Alternative Agriculture*, Vol.1, No.4, pp.169–73.

McCay, B.M. and J.M. Acheson (eds.), 1987, *The Question of the Commons: the Culture and Ecology of Communal Resources*, Tucson, AZ: University of Arizona Press.

Marsh, G.P., 1864, *Man and Nature*, New York: Scribner (reprinted 1965, with an introduction by D. Lowenthal, Cambridge, MA: Belknap Press).

Martinez-Alier, J. (with Klaus Schlupmann, 1987, *Ecological Economics: Energy, Environment and Society*, Oxford: Basil Blackwell.

Meadows, D.H., Meadows, D.L., Randers, J. and W.W. Behrens, 1972, *The Limits to Growth: A Report for the Club of Rome's Project on the Predicament of Mankind*, London and New York: Earth Island Press and Universe Press.

Mill, J.S., 1848/1970, *Principles of Political Economy*, Boston, MA: Charles C. Little and James Brown (Reprinted, 1970, edited by D. Winch, Harmondsworth: Penguin Books).

Mishan, E. J., 1977, *The Economic Growth Debate: An Assessment*, London: Allen & Unwin.

Nye, P.H. and D.J. Greenland, 1960, *The Soil Under Shifting Cultivation*, Technical Communication No. 51, Commonwealth Bureau of Soils, Harpenden, UK: Commonwealth Agricultural Bureaux.

O'Riordan, T., 1981, *Environmentalism* (second edition), London: Pion Press.

O'Riordan, T., 1988, 'The Politics of Sustainability', in R.K. Turner (ed.), *Sustainable Environmental Management: Principles and Practice*, London: Bellhaven Press and Boulder, CO: Westview Press, pp.29–50.

O'Riordan, T. and R.K. Turner, 1983, *An Annotated Reader in Environmental Planning and Management*, Oxford: Pergamon Press.

Parikh, J.K., 1988, 'Sustainable Development of Agricultural Systems: Concerns, Approaches and Policy Insights', in J.K. Parikh (ed.), *Sustainable Development in Agriculture*, Dordrecht: Martinus Nijhoff Publishers, pp.367–79.

Passmore, J., 1974, *Man's Responsibility for Nature*, London: Duckworth.

Pavelis, G.A., 1983, 'Conservation Capital in the United States, 1935–1980', *Journal of Soil and Water Conservation*, Vol.38, No.6, pp.455–58.

Pearce, D.W., 1976, *Environmental Economics*, New York: Longman.

Pearce, D.W., 1988, 'The Sustainable Use of Natural Resources in Developing Countries', in R.K. Turner (ed.), *Sustainable Environmental Management: Principles and Practice*, London: Bellhaven Press and Boulder, CO: Westview Press, pp.102–17.

Pearce, D.W., Markandya, A. and E.B. Barbier, 1989, *Blueprint for a Green Economy, a Report for the UK Department of the Environment*, London: Earthscan Publications.

Pearce, D.W. and R.K. Turner, 1990, *Economics of Natural Resources and the Environment*, Hemel Hempstead, UK: Harvester Wheatsheaf.

Pearce, D.W., Barbier, E.B. and A. Markandya, 1990, *Sustainable Development: Economics and Environment in the Third World*, Aldershot, UK: Edward Elgar.

Perrings, C., 1987, *Economy and Environment: A Theoretical Essay on the Interdependence of Economic and Environmental Systems*, Cambridge: Cambridge University Press.

Pezzey, J., 1988, 'Market Mechanisms of Pollution Control: 'Polluter Pays', Economic and Practical Aspects', in R.K. Turner (ed.), *Sustainable Environmental Management: Principles and Practice*, London: Bellhaven Press and Boulder, CO: Westview Press, pp.190–242.

Porter, D., B.J. Allen, and G. Thompson, 1991, *Development in Practice: Paved with Good Intentions*, London: Routledge.

Redclift, M., 1987, *Sustainable Development: Exploring the Contradictions*, London and New York: Methuen.

Richards, P., 1985, *Indigenous Agricultural Revolution*, London: Hutchinson.

Riddell, R., 1981, *Ecodevelopment: Economics, Ecology and Development: An Alternative to Growth Imperative Models*, Farnborough, UK: Gower.

Ruthenberg, H., 1980, *Farming Systems in the Tropics* (third edition), Oxford: Clarendon Press.
Sachs, I., 1976, 'Environment and Styles of Development', in W.H. Matthews (ed.), *Outer Limits and Human Needs*, Uppsala: Dag Hammarskjold Foundation, pp.41–65.
Sachs, I., 1984, 'The Strategies of Ecodevelopment', *Ceres (FAO Review on Agriculture and Development)*, Vol.17, No.4, pp.17–21.
Sherratt. A., 1980, 'Water, Soil and Seasonality in Early Cereal Cultivation', *World Archaeology*, Vol.11, No.3, pp.313–30.
Simon, D., 1989, 'Sustainable Development: Theoretical Construct or Attainable Goal?', *Environmental Conservation*, Vol.16, No.1, pp.41–8.
Simon, J.L. and H. Kahn (eds.), 1984, *The Resourceful Earth: A Response to Global 2000*, New York: Basil Blackwell.
Singer, M., 1987, *Passage to a Human World*, Indianapolis, IN: Hudson Institute.
Smil, V., 1987, *Energy – Food – Environment: Realities – Myths – Options*, Oxford: Clarendon Press.
Solow, R.M., 1971, 'The Economist's Approach to Pollution Control', *Science*, Vol.173, No.3996, pp.498–503.
Solow, R.M., 1974, 'Intergenerational Equity and Exhaustible Resources', *Review of Economic Studies*, Vol.41, Supplement, pp.29–45.
Toye, J., 1987, *Dilemmas of Development: Reflections on the Counter-Revolution in Development Theory and Policy*, Oxford: Basil Blackwell.
Turner, R.K. (ed.), 1988, *Sustainable Environmental Management: Principles and Practice*, London: Bellhaven Press and Boulder, CO: Westview Press.
Turner, R. K., 1988, 'Sustainability, Resource Conservation and Pollution Control: An Overview', in R. K. Turner (ed.), *Sustainable Environmental Management: Principles and Practice*, London: Bellhaven Press and Boulder, CO: Westview Press, pp.1–25.
Ul Haq, M., 1976, *The Poverty Curtain: Choices for the Third World*, New York: Columbia University Press.
Underwood, D.A. and P.G. King, 1989, 'On the Ideological Foundations of Environmental Policy', *Ecological Economics*, Vol.1, No.4, pp.315–34.
Unger, P.W. and T.M. McCalla, 1980, 'Conservation Tillage Systems', *Advances in Agronomy*, Vol.33, pp.1–58.
Wilkinson, R.G., 1973, *Poverty and Progress: An Ecological Model of Economic Development*, London: Methuen.
World Commission [on Environment and Development], 1987, *Our Common Future*, Oxford and New York: Oxford University Press.
Wynne-Edwards, V.C., 1962, *Animal Dispersion in Relation to Social Behaviour*, New York: Hafner.

Sustainable Development

Sukhatmoy Chakravarty

Editorial Note:

This must be one of Professor Chakravarty's last public statements, for shortly after the Oslo Conference he returned to India, where he fell ill and died on 22 August 1990, finally succumbing to a heart condition which had troubled him for many years. Professor Chakravarty had intended to revise this speech for publication, but in the circumstances we are publishing his text with only minor editorial changes. It is an honour for us to publish this sadly valedictory speech by one of the foremost development economists of his day. Sukhatmoy Chakravarty was at home both in technical and policy discussion, and his knowledge ranged far afield in history, politics and sociology, apart from economics. He was a kindly man and gave of his time to all sorts of people who approached him. He had become a welcome and familiar figure in the world of Development Economics and he is sadly missed by many friends all over the world.

I

'Sustainable development' is a much discussed topic these days. One need only glance at recent literature on global developmental issues to conclude that it is a concept which appeals to many, especially to those who are a bit fed up with yesterday's talk of ever-increasing levels of consumption over time. Even those countries which have seen very little increase in consumption per capita are attracted to this concept because of population growth, unbalanced urbanisation and accompanying threats to their natural resource endowments. It would thus appear that here is a concept which can form the basis of a new development consensus, akin to but somewhat different in character from the consensus that prevailed during the 1950s and 1960s of this century. Indeed recent reports such as the Brundtland Report have highlighted precisely this concept as the key unifying element behind the need for refashioning development strategies in the 1990s and beyond.

Despite what it is currently fashionable to claim, I do not believe that an earlier generation of development planners and policy makers made a fetish of 'growth rates' and very few ever talked of a maximum rate of growth as the 'optimal rate of growth', even when the concept was deployed in a purely analytic sense. None the less I believe that the present emphasis on 'sustainable development' is welcome for several reasons. First, it places environmental concerns squarely in the centre of discussion, an emphasis that was sadly missing in many earlier discussions where a dichotomy was inserted between the needs of development and the maintenance of environmental resources. Secondly, while the earlier line of thinking may have led many in the poorer countries to believe that they could afford to wait for environment-improving measures till they had achieved a reasonable level of living defined in terms of conventional baskets of goods and services, the present thinking would suggest that this was a mistake. There is little doubt that in terms of food and nutrition standards, a majority of the world's population live in situations of extreme deprivation and hence growth in a conventional sense is desirable.

However, it cannot be denied that the very process of bringing improvements in environmental policy can block off future development possibilities in the 'levels of living' which is a more inclusive concept of welfare. This is because growth in a conventional sense can use up too much 'space' or lead to an excessively fast depletion of exhaustible (or non-renewable) resource, or disrupt traditional life styles by placing an undue emphasis on marketed commodities and services. All such developments may only lead to a temporary increase in the 'levels of living' of a few generations and some privileged social strata within a given generation, while the prospects before the rest may well be made bleaker as a result.

Technically put, the argument here is that economic equilibria are often path-dependent, making it obligatory for us to take a critical and non-myopic look at decision processes about how much to consume and invest, and also at the possible replacement of assets which have been used up. Part of the problem arises from the fact that conventional economic theory has dealt with a highly restrictive concept of the 'production boundary'. While classical economists like Smith emphasised a 'materialist approach' to production for reasons which were based on their preoccupation with 'capital accumulation' under early capitalism, subsequent widening of the concept in the hands of neo-classical economists placed an undue emphasis on the 'marketability' of the items entering into national income accounts. This implied that for commodities or services where markets did not exist or could not be run on a profit maximising basis, no corresponding entries needed to be made in preparing the final table of contents relating to the end-products of economic activities.

Alfred Marshall and even more his great successor at Cambridge, Arthur Cecil Pigou, were very much aware that this procedure provided only a partial picture of the level of wellbeing of a nation. Pigou was notable for the emphasis that he placed on the necessity to introduce corrections to market prices so as to get a more accurate measure of real resource cost on the margin – if external effects were duly recognised. But, even he did not feel the need at that time to introduce a system of 'resource cost accounting' to indicate that developments under a market regime imply using up stocks of non-renewable resources whose changing scarcity values were not reflected in a profile of rising market prices. Hotelling's subsequent paper on the 'optimal rate of depletion of exhaustible resources' seemed to suggest that suitably time-weighted market prices – weighting being done with respect to either the market 'interest rate' or a social rate of discount – could ensure that economies do not 'overexploit' these resources.

We now seem to agree that the conventional approach based on the 'Hotelling rule' is not adequate to deal with the possibility of welfare losses over time which may arise from too fast a rate of exhaustion of our 'natural resource endowment'. In other words, we seem to be implying that a price-interest regime cannot by itself cope with all the pertinent issues. There is a large body of literature now which deals with the strength and limitations of Hotelling's rule. Since they have been reviewed elsewhere in the literature, I do not feel that it is necessary to summarise it here. It is, however, pertinent to point out that at the back of much current discussion by mainstream economists, there is an implicit assumption that 'exhaustible resources, on the margin can be effectively substituted by means of man-made capital equipment or by superior technology. While such an assumption may sometimes be correct, and may in fact suggest occasionally promising lines of action, there may well exist threshold phenomena beyond which such an extrapolation may indeed be very hazardous.

I have so far dealt with the inefficiency of market regimes in dealing with exhaustible resources. Unfavourable experience in economies where methods of central planning based on public ownership of land and means of production had been practised over decades, would suggest that mistakes have been committed precisely in these areas of natural resource management where the long view could have been taken by central planners who should have been less subject to the rapacity of the present, as Harrod once put it. It is possible that similarities in outcome amongst different economic regimes have arisen from ignoring certain fundamental irreversible processes which require a different conceptualisation of the development process.

It is necessary to be precise about the expression 'irreversible' at this stage. It means that there are critical factors, which once disturbed from their 'normal values' cannot be easily restored to their original positions through substitution by additional human efforts or by means of manmade machines and 'artificial' materials. While some scholars such as Georgescu-Roegen and his disciple Rifkin would ultimately trace it all back to the all-pervasive second law of thermodynamics, we do not need to take such a fundamentalist position to appreciate the essential point that for practical purposes, 'irreversibility' has to be judged in relation to the resources effectively available to different countries at different stages of development and in a few critical areas to the planet as a whole. Many environmentalists would insist that there is strong evidence to suggest that for the planet as a whole, we are fast approaching a singular situation.

There is a great deal of contemporary discussion on the 'greenhouse effect' leading to 'global warming', depletion of the ozone layer, loss of bio-diversity, which would suggest that development along current lines could not continue beyond a certain point of time, well within the thinking span of contemporary humanity. I have no doubt that despite great diversity of opinions on matters of detail, there is a lot of substance in the fears that are currently being expressed. For example, in an article in *Nature*, the Columbia University Professor, Wallace S. Broecker, wrote: 'we play Russian roulette with climate [and] no one knows what lies in the active chamber of the gun' [*Nature 328-9: 123-6*]. The crucial question would be whether the changes taking place are slowly cumulative, even if not reversible, or whether they can move in a discontinuous fashion. We are well aware that there exist dynamic systems where changes in parameters build up into drastically changed scenarios. If the probability of abrupt change exists, as many suggest, then substitutions induced through normal market mechanisms or through slowly moving bureaucracies may be completely inadequate or in some cases may even compound the problems they seek to solve.

Even if we were to temporarily suspend our judgements on these long-term changes which may be irreversible as well as discontinuous, a look at the world at large would suggest that for the majority of inhabitants on the earth the precariousness of their daily existence has not been significantly reduced by the development process even where there have been increases in per capita GNP. This is in part due to the fact of population increase which has been due less to an improvement in living conditions than to improvements in medical technology which have eliminated certain dreaded diseases of the past. Neither new technology nor investment in material capital have enabled them to substitute for the loss of their environmental capital stock which has been seriously eroded. The situation has been rendered more difficult by the imitation of an alien life-style especially by the elite in these countries.

I can, therefore, easily see two major reasons why discussion on sustainable development should become a topic of great interest. One is the growing fact of interdependence which leads to international external effects which are not compensated for by appropriate price response and resource shifts. Secondly, the distributional aspects of contemporary growth processes have been far from uniform, leading to excess consumption by some accompanied by widespread hunger and malnutrition on the part of others. It is clear from these two reasons alone that sustainable development brings into sharper focus issues which were either ignored or insufficiently emphasised in an earlier stage of development discussion.

II

How should we proceed in devising a development strategy which focuses attention on sustainability? For some people, sustainable development simply implies a lower rate of growth of gross national product as conventionally measured. For a few others, sustainability would require that goods and services should not be valued at their current market prices but only after proper care has been taken to net out the costs of natural resources used up, which are not currently available for market exchange, even when they are essential for carrying out production at existing or increasing levels.

A blanket recommendation to lower the target rate of growth of output would be hardly appropriate or adequate as circumstances vary widely amongst different countries. For countries where per capita income levels are a mere fraction of what is being enjoyed in the more developed parts of the world, howsoever measured, and where basic necessities are scarcely available to nearly three quarters of the population, a recommendation to slow down the rate of GNP growth, despite all the limitations that attach to the concept, would go against the very spirit of sustainable development. There is little doubt that poverty often forces populations in these countries to draw upon their environmental capital in a manner which makes their future living conditions more precarious. We are often told about the vast extent of land degradation, and deforestation which are currently taking place in South Asia or the extent of desertification in Sub-Saharan Africa, or rapid destruction of tropical forests in the Amazon region. These are processes which in many cases have caused changes which may prove well nigh irreversible or reversible only at high cost which local communities cannot be expected to meet. We are noticing in these cases a depletion of 'social wealth' which if properly measured may imply negative real growth in income in the Fisherian sense of the term. Sustainable development in these situations would suggest appropriate induction of technology, know – how and material capital which can enable the population to reach higher standards of living while maintaining their 'natural capital' more or less intact.

No doubt to put such a solution into practice would prove extremely difficult. There are both internal as well as international obstacles to such a programme which cannot be ignored, an issue I shall return to later.

At the other end of the development spectrum, we have countries where standards of living are characterised by over-consumption of goods and services, which are causing irreversible long run damage to the environment, even when, on the face of it they would appear to be free from overt signs of environmental degradation. Very high levels of CFC consumption, or of liquid hydrocarbon use in one form or another, are examples which have been frequently cited in recent years as demanding changes in life style and in the composition of goods and services produced. Using the capacity to pay as the determinant of choice and their vast ability to modify technology and capital equipment, given their intellectual and material infrastructure, these countries may, even in a market-directed regime, move over to a 'sustainable growth path' were it not the case that the globe has become much too interdependent, a point that scientists continually stress upon us. International externalities are these days such powerful facts of life that it would be foolish to expect that current differential patterns of growth can coexist for long, without doing serious harm to the global community in the years to come. This point has been so well developed in recent literature that it is unnecessary to elaborate on it here. Clearly, what is needed is a greater clarity on what to do in the next couple of decades.

It is fairly obvious that poorer countries must be enabled to grow at rates which are fast enough to bring about perceptible changes in levels of living, even as they are asked to bring down their rates of population growth. In order that such a transition may be speeded up, technological changes in areas of energy transition, including research aimed at improving productivity of grain and tree crops in non-temperate regions would require very urgent attention. The same argument would apply to eradication of diseases which are especially endemic in these areas. Secondly, resources released through reduced production of arms, should find their way into augmenting productive capacity where such augmentation is urgently needed. Keynes once deplored the fact that it was a great pity that politics as conventionally understood did not permit societies to plan for expenditure on the level needed to confirm the validity of his theory excepting during times of war. Now that we can hope the cold war will diminish at least in intensity, it would be a pity if maintenance of effective demand in developed countries required expanded production programmes for relatively unessential items of daily life when the vast majority of the world have to go without their daily bread.

In recent years, there has grown up an attitude of mind which finds all solutions to lie in the area of market directed processes. It tends to emphasise private flow of capital as against official development assistance, protection of intellectual property rights as the sure source of generating new technology, and an open door policy to imports of goods and services for countries whose terms of trade have declined, partly because world demand for the raw materials they were producing has shifted. To a certain extent, this may reflect an element of disenchantment with an earlier strategy of development. It is possible to share some of it, even when one would regard the newly found wisdom to be seriously detrimental to the continued health of the world economy. Allocative efficiency is indeed a virtue which one should not underrate. That resources may have been inefficiently utilised in the past is surely an argument for doing better. But economists will understand the issue better if I were to say that the path towards a theoretically defined Pareto-optimal state need not in itself be Pareto-imposing. Clearly, therefore traditional strategies which take effective notice of distributional considerations, intranationally and internationally, will have to be devised.

III

Apart from the global issues analysed earlier, the strategy of 'sustainable development' in the context of developing countries encompasses several issues at the national level. It would be over-simple to view it as a problem which could be solved by limitation on population growth or restraint of consumption on the part of the affluent sections of the society. Much as we desire restraint on both these processes, the issues involved are much more complex. Environmental degradation in the developing countries has resulted from the combined impact of demographic pressures, the types of development strategies pursued, including some of their unintended consequences and the nature of public policies adopted in the course of development planning.

In many poor countries, the operation of market forces in certain spheres of economic activity along with the impact of interventionist policies in terms of development priorities and pricing of goods and services have been instrumental in accentuating environmental degradation. While it may be difficult to segregate the magnitude of environmental damage caused by market forces from that caused by public policies, one can easily provide numerous illustrations for both.

Many poor countries tend to have fairly high rates of population growth because of a number of socio-economic characteristics whose origin could be traced to their traditional patterns of livelihood, family life, settlement, community beliefs and customs, not to speak of other factors such as lack of access to education and primary health care. There is some evidence to show that the demographic transition has just begun in certain countries of South Asia and this process can be further accelerated through suitable policy planning and additional expansion of health care facilities. On the other hand, it would be unrealistic to expect a similar process to get under way in Sub-Saharan Africa within the same time frame. The Latin American countries should be in an even better position than the South Asian countries in this respect, provided the social stability widely disrupted during the eighties returns there quickly enough.

Thus, it would be unrealistic to expect population in the poorer parts of the world to stabilise before the third decade of the coming century. What makes the problem more complicated is that the process of demographic transition cannot be accelerated by pressing down current consumption per capita, if only for purely biomedical reasons. It is in this context that the type of development strategies and the nature of public policies pursued in the developing countries assume great importance.

Given the demographic pressure and the constraints of land resources, agricultural development strategy in most developing countries has emphasised the role of expanding irrigation, increased use of chemical fertilisers and pesticides as well as the adoption of high yielding varieties (HYV) of cereals and other crops with a view to increase the productivity per unit of land. While this strategy has definitely helped in increasing agricultural production, especially foodgrain production, doubts are now expressed in many quarters whether this process can be sustained any longer in the absence of effective measures for maintaining ecological stability.

There is a growing realisation that the periodic set-backs to agricultural production witnessed in different parts of the world due to natural calamities such as floods and droughts have been caused by factors such as deforestation and lack of appropriate measures for soil and water conservation in the course of development. There is a growing awareness about the critical role that forests play in maintaining ecological stability, but unfortunately poor land use practices and deforestation in many developing countries are undermining the supportive role of forests. There is enough evidence to show that the useful lifetime of many irrigation dams and hydroelectric reservoirs may be drastically reduced at the sedimentation rates currently observed in various countries stretching from the Philippines to Brazil and Costa Rica.

In other words, it appears that the development strategy pursued so far has itself set in motion an unsustainable development process, which has further been accentuated by certain public policies such as pricing/subsidies for intermediate inputs like fertilisers, pesticides, irrigation water and electricity as well as provision of cheap capital. This process, however, can be prevented from causing further ecological damage if we are able to initiate appropriate policies for reversing this process. This would require efforts not just in terms of market forces versus public intervention, but more in terms of institutional changes.

Common property resources such as forests, grazing land, irrigation tanks, water courses or field channels in irrigation systems, etc., have traditionally been maintained in developing countries through community participation at the village level. However, with the advent of development planning and the growing influence of market forces, the involvement of the local communities in the maintenance of common property resources has broken down. This implies that in the present context greater attention needs to be given to the institutional aspects of maintaining common property resources. Furthermore, changes in the institutional mechanism cannot succeed without a proper system of economic incentives and disincentives. Public policies in this regard have, therefore, to address themselves to the needs of the local population who have certain expectations in terms of both short and long-term gains.

To reconcile such interests, it is necessary to adopt some innovative approaches. For example, it is reported that Nepal had successfully adopted a strategy for rehabilitating uplands by transferring control of forest lands from the government to local communities and paying them for planting trees and fodder crops which provided the people with the incentive to involve themselves in the programme. Without such changes in the institutional arrangements, reafforestation programmes may not succeed even if sufficient resources are allocated for this purpose. In this context, it has to be realised that poverty is one of the important causes for deforestation. It is the growing pressure on land which leads to encroachments on forests. It may, therefore, be necessary to formulate development strategies that are less land-intensive such as animal husbandry, fisheries, etc., that could provide earning opportunities for the rural poor. Thus, the protection of environmental and reforestation programmes must go along with programmes for the uplift of the rural poor.

As stated earlier, agricultural development strategies have laid greater emphasis on the introduction of new technologies and commercialisation of agriculture, while institutional reforms have almost been neglected. This process has led to unequal distribution of the benefits and costs. Big farmers have enjoyed the benefits of subsidies on inputs like fertilisers, pesticides, electricity and irrigation water, while the sharing of the benefits from increased productivity between the land owners, farm labour and the consumer has been relegated to the background in the fixing of farm support prices. Such policies have led to an indiscriminate and wasteful use of resources while aggravating environmental damage. It is in this context that we may have to do some rethinking about the continued pursuit of new technologies as well as the pricing/subsidy policies.

Agricultural practices based on biological interactions, instead of chemicals, may require greater attention. Currently, prospects for bio-technology are difficult to assess. As and when they succeed, it is likely that gains would accrue disproportionately to those countries which have the greatest R&D capabilities, even when their levels of productivity are already high in many areas. In principle, they could also lead to considerable improvement in developing countries, but in practice, much will depend on the areas where research is focused as well as on the terms and conditions on which new technologies based on greater knowledge are transmitted to the recipients in developing countries.

For achieving sustainable development, public policies have also to pay greater attention to the energy needs of the large mass of the poor living in the rural areas whose energy demands are not reflected in the commercial energy market. While expansion of electricity to interior rural areas might have helped in satisfying the energy needs for purposes such as lighting, pumping irrigation water, etc., this process has not helped in meeting the critical energy needs for cooking purposes in the rural areas. The search for new energy sources, especially renewable ones, has therefore assumed importance on the agenda of development planning. Energy sources such as solar, wind, biogas and biomass have all become prominent because these sources help sustain the development process without producing an adverse impact on environmental conditions. The adoption of these new sources of energy on a large scale would very much depend upon the economic viability and easy availability of these sources. In addition, there are also various technological, institutional and social issues involved in the large-scale adoption of these new sources.

In the Indian context, the use of biogas energy seems to have made much more rapid progress as compared to solar and wind energy systems. More than a million biogas plants are functioning in India, mostly in rural areas. Further spread of these plants has been hampered by various problems such as their cost, availability of raw materials, distribution of product/byproduct, etc. Co-operative management of community biogas plants at the village level has not spread to many States in India. On the other hand, the cost of individual plants is quite high, and this can be reduced only through intensive efforts to develop more economical designs of digesters, burners and biogas engines. While public policies have to pay greater attention to the institutional aspects, modern technology can help in designing more cost-effective energy systems.

IV

While modern technology is a help, it cannot work unaided in this any more than in other spheres. Technology is a part of man's exosmotic evolution, a feature specific to human species as pointed out by Alfred

Lotka a long time ago. Some have read deeply pessimistic meanings into this characteristic that Lotka discerned nearly 70 years ago, including the basis for intra-specific conflict. It is also possible to look at it from a more optimistic angle. While, as of now, arguments for pessimism and optimism are evenly balanced, a major change in perspective can be brought about only if mankind were made to realise their common stake.

As of now, there would appear to be great reluctance to recognise that these common stakes would suggest a very different approach to major issues relating to transfer of capital, labour and know-how. Internationalisation in communication and transportation has been accompanied by very patchy improvements in production capacity. While productivity growth rates amongst the developed countries have tended to converge, the difference between developed and developing countries has, by and large, widened. This has implied the growing payments deficits by the developing world, aided and abetted no doubt by the short sighted policies pursued by its own elite. If we indict them for utilising the emotional forces of nationalism in a self-serving manner, we have to reckon with the fact that no transnational mechanism is available as of now which can be expected to take better care of the poor in the vast majority of these countries. Similarly, in the countries of the developed world, there is a generally prevailing perception that they owe their prosperity only to their superior knowledge, management capabilities and prevalence of a higher moral code relating to interpersonal transactions.

A thorough change in currently held attitudes is an essential prerequisite to sustainable development. Our response patterns are still largely shaped by the material circumstances which prevailed a century ago. Modern technological developments, while highly uneven in their impact, have changed objective circumstances all around. A throwback to a system of *laissez-faire* which may have briefly prevailed in the nineteenth century can no longer work, because of the growth of interdependence in production, consumption and communication amongst nations. Multilateral coordination of economic and social policies has become an imperative necessity for efficient and equitable management of the lives of planets' inhabitants. 'Sustainable development' is, therefore, a concept which has a vast reach. We have not yet fully explored it even on the conceptual level let alone worked out a practicable programme of action.

The 'Non-Polluter Gets Paid' Principle for Third World Commodity Exports

Henk L.M. Kox*

INTRODUCTION

The report of the World Commission on Environment and Development, better known as the Brundtland report, has been a prominent eye-opener with regard to the dual relation between environment and development. It points out how economic growth and the quality of growth are influenced by the ecological issue. Besides, it shows how ecological devastation in many developing countries is amplified by poverty-led behaviour and by the need to secure foreign exchange. Production of primary export commodities is often linked with environmental damage. The current debt situation and adjustment policies force countries to increase their production of export commodities with concomitant further pressure on the biophysical environment. It is for this reason that the Commission expressed 'the need for more effective instruments to integrate environment and development concerns into international trading patterns' [*WCED, 1987: 84*].

It becomes increasingly clear that environmental degradation does not respect national borders. From the present state of knowledge about a number of global environmental problems – a weakening 'green lung' capacity of tropical rain forests, perforation of the ozone layer and global warming, dwindling of species, and pollution of oceans with potential far-reaching implications for oxygen production by plankton – it emerges that international co-ordination and action is urgently needed. It is likely that the 1990s will see an intensification of attempts to integrate costs of environmental preservation and natural resource use in regular international price systems.

This article argues that the creation of such an economic instrument is feasible for the most important export sector of developing countries, namely exports of primary commodities to OECD countries. This economic device, labelled *International Commodity and Environment Agreement*,

*Revised version of paper presented to the 6th EADI General Conference in Oslo, June 1990. Faculty of Economics and Econometrics, Section Development Economics, Free University, De Boelelaan 1105, 1081 HV Amsterdam, Netherlands. The author thanks Hans Linnemann and Cor Wattel for useful comments on earlier versions of this study.

builds upon the remnants of 'traditional' commodity agreements but, unlike the latter, is not concerned with price stabilisation. It aims primarily at integration of environmental externalities in the commodity prices paid

by OECD countries. Before describing this instrument, some attention will be given to ecological damage associated with Third World production of export commodities, to attempts to evaluate this damage, and to theoretical insights on integration of environmental externalities in price systems.

PRODUCTION OF EXPORT COMMODITIES AND ENVIRONMENT

The period of low prices since 1980 urged many countries to produce and export larger volumes of primary commodities in order to finance their import needs and debt. Prescriptions to increase commodity exports often formed part of the IMF readjustment package for countries with debt problems, thus contributing to further international supply imbalance and depression of export commodity prices. In a basic policy document on Sub-Saharan Africa the World Bank calls on these countries to increase their commodity exports in spite of depressed world markets.[1] Export diversification programmes are difficult to realise and can work only in the longer term. Many countries tried to shift towards downstream activities in the production chain (industrial processing of primary products) in order to improve their export earnings. Slow progress in this field can partly be explained by a limited propensity to invest in these activities by foreign companies, by technological problems, by the structure of international marketing and distribution of processed commodities, and in some cases, by tariff escalation in OECD countries. In the foreseeable future commodity production remains a vital export sector for a vast majority of developing countries.[2]

Some ecological effects of production of primary commodities have become a matter of international concern by now. This holds for the destructive effects of deforestation in the Amazon region and in South-East Asia. Most of this damage is caused by export of tropical hardwood logs, production of mineral resources with export destinations, and extensive cattle ranching, mostly producing for meat exports.[3] According to the FAO agricultural extension for export-oriented agroindustry (for example, groundnuts) may account for 70 per cent of Sub-Saharan deforestation [*Le Prestre, 1989: 170*]. Cattle ranching for export of meat or live animals is also a cause of overgrazing and soil erosion in many arid zones [*Myers and Tucker, 1987*]. Over-intense fishing of coastal waters and deep sea areas, often by international fishery companies, negatively affects the regeneration capacity of these ecospheres. Sometimes it devastates the coral reefs and the sea bottom [*Swaminathan, 1987*].

The production of cash crops like soya, cocoa, coffee, cotton, tobacco, rubber, and sugar cane is often linked with abundant use of chemical fertilisers and pesticides, especially when production units are large. Often forests are destroyed by agricultural extension to grow these products. Intensive use of agrochemicals contributes heavily to pollution of the subsoil and surface waters. Moreover, it has cumulative long-term effects in the form of pesticide residuals in animal and human food chains, a diminishing biodiversity, soil erosion and falling ground water levels. The latter two consequences are in their turn important causes of desertification [*Redclift, 1989; Barbier, 1989; Mortimore, 1989; Van Amstel et al., 1986; Pearce et al., 1990*).

Export mining also contributes to soil erosion by demolition of vegetation and soil structure, especially in the case of open-cast mining (copper, tin, zinc, bauxite). Other metal mining activities create giant waste heaps or dispose of toxic wastes and polluted run-off [*Blunden, 1985*].

Ecological effects of commodity production are felt mostly by the local population in producing countries, either directly or in the long run. Lagged effects such as soil erosion, or exhaustion of soil and water resources, manifest themselves through regular 'natural' catastrophes (land slides, floods, large forest fires, or drought). Similarly, they may appear in the form of a slow process of falling agricultural yields, causing rural impoverishment, departure for urban shanty towns, and depopulation of rural areas. Direct economic consequences of deforestation are not confined to the depletion of future timber sources. It also produces the disappearance of non-timber means of existence for the local populations like medicinal and aromatic herbs, barks (for example, quinquina), fibres, flowers, resins, fats, and other forest products. Only a small part of harmful ecological side effects of commodity production trickles down along the international trade chain to the commodity-importing countries. This may have the form of residues of pesticides, herbicides or fungicides in agricultural commodities. These make themselves felt as health hazards for harbour, transport and manufacturing workers and, ultimately, also for consumers in importing countries.

Other, less direct effects of large-scale environmental degradation in developing countries, like those mentioned in the introduction, are only recently receiving international attention. These long-term, cumulative effects are transnational in character and can only be tackled by international co-operation.

VALUATION OF DAMAGE

If environmental externalities of export production are to be integrated in international commodity prices, exercises to quantify the costs of environmental degradation in the monetary dimension are indispensable. Several methods exist for measuring the costs of environmental damage. Each offers a different approach for tackling the quantification problems. Three central problems arise. First, ecological effects have no natural unit of measurement. This specially applies to influence on amenities. Second, environmental effects have the character both of externalities and of public goods: they represent no private property, are not sold in markets and their value cannot be assessed in a direct way. The third and perhaps most important issue is that ecological effects, due to their complexity, uncertainty, and to our far from complete knowledge about the complex ecosystems, can hardly be forecasted [*Turner, 1988*]. Non-linearity of ecological relations means that sudden vehement reactions can occur due to small, gradual changes.[4]

Some methods base their estimates upon valuations derived from revealed or stated preferences of individual consumers [*Nash and Bowers, 1988*]. Because of the public goods character of ecological effects such valuation efforts seem less appropriate. Moreover, using these methods assumes a large degree of discretionary consumer choice, which is scarcely available at the low absolute income levels prevailing in most developing nations. Preferences are influenced by income and knowledge levels, not only between individuals, but also between nations. Even if 'The Polluter Pays', the permission to dump heavily polluted chemical waste in a poor African country is probably more a function of income and knowledge than a function of 'autonomous' preferences. The willingness-to-be-compensated is therefore a dangerous standard for ecological valuation attempts in situations where large differences in income and knowledge about long-term effects prevail.

The method mostly applied for measuring environmental effects in developing countries is the *alternative costs* method. Basically, it tries to valuate unpriced production or resource consumption by using related economic variables that already do have a price at this moment, though sometimes in a different economic space [*Ahmad, 1981; Hufschmidt and Hyman, 1982*]. With regard to environmental costs of primary export production two variants of this method have been used.

The first variant basically counts the costs of environmental preservation that would have been incurred *if* the same production would have been undertaken in some other country with more advanced environmental regulations. Often the reference country is the United States. What is

being measured, therefore, is primarily the amount of economised costs.[5]
By not demanding or by not being able to maintain the same ecological
standards developing countries in fact subsidise industries and consumers
in OECD countries. Walter and Loudon [*1986*] calculated that OECD
countries for their 1980 imports from developing countries would have
incurred direct pollution control costs of $5.5 billion if they had been
required to meet the environmental standards then prevailing in the United
States. If the pollution control expenditures associated with the materials
that went into the final product are also counted, the costs would have
mounted to $14.2 billion in 1980. In the same years Third World exports
of non-oil commodities to developed market economies amounted to $68
billion [*UNCTAD, 1990b*], so that it is fair to speak of a considerable
hidden subsidy. For two reasons the aforementioned amounts under-
estimate the 'real' costs of ecological damage. First, because they do
not count costs associated with resource depletion, and secondly because
cost-price increasing environmental regulations in the reference country
do not cover all ecological damage. Total ecological costs are, therefore,
a multiple of the aforementioned amounts. Ironically, this very ecological
'comparative cost advantage' of Third World exporters is an argument for
OECD producers to demand protectionist measures against these imports
[*Ford and Runge, 1990*]. In the Uruguay Round of GATT negotiations the
use of environmental protectionism has been widely discussed.

A second application of the 'alternative costs' method tries to evaluate
ecological damage by counting the commercial costs which will be incurred
when the destroyed environment has to be reshaped in its original condition.
Estimates have been made of total costs of timber extraction and forest
conversion in Indonesia during 1982. Cost elements include depreciation of
the forest stock, costs of timber extraction itself (including logging damage
and fires), and foregone costs of minor forest products. In Repetto, Wells
et al. [*1987*] these costs have been estimated at a total of $3.1 billion, or
about four per cent of Indonesian GDP that year. This estimate has been
criticised as being too low.[6] Several studies quantify the cost effects of soil
erosion in developing countries [*Dasgupta and Maeler, 1989*]. Production
of export commodities is a major, but, of course, not the only cause of soil
erosion.[7] The United Nations Environment Programme (UNEP) estimated
the total global cost effects of desertification in arid zones at $26 billion
annually as a consequence of lost agricultural and livestock productivity
[*Mortimore, 1989*]. In Mali foregone farmers' incomes due to soil erosion
are estimated at $31–123 million annually, which is equal to 4–16
per cent of agricultural GDP [*Bishop and Allen, 1989*]. On-site costs of
soil erosion in upland areas in Java are estimated to amount $320 million
annually, or three per cent of agricultural GDP. Counting the costs caused

by downstream sedimentation of eroded soils would add another $25–90 million [*Magrath and Arens, 1987*].

Both variants of the alternative costs method can be criticised in some respects. In case of the first method one could remark that a perfect counterfactual case does not exist, so that additional adjustments have to be made. In case of the second method it is obvious that ecological damage will never be solely caused by production of primary export commodities. Moreover, cost-benefit methods usually treat irreversible environmental effects of projects no differently from more reversible effects, and the practice of using cost-benefit methods has therefore been criticised for strongly favouring projects with short-term benefits and long-term costs (as is often the case for environmental effects) [*Goodland and Ledec, 1987*].

Even though some criticism is possible, the estimates made it plausible that ecological costs of commodity production are substantial and that the magnitude of the hidden environmental subsidy transferred to OECD countries, is far from trivial. This would justify an integration of environmental externalities in international commodity prices to be based not only on ecological and/or solidarity grounds, but also on economic grounds.

CURES AND GROWTH PRIORITIES

Abatement of ecological devastation in commodity producing countries has both a stock and a flow aspect. The stock aspects centers around the arrears in ecological 'reparations'. The flow aspect concentrates on the modalities of a different growth model that incorporates ecological preservation at an ongoing basis, while depletion of non-renewable resources is minimised.

Repair of ecological damage caused by production of primary export commodities in past years will require ample funds for environmental reconstruction and protection. At a national level such funds have more and more come into existence in OECD countries. At an international scale large financial efforts are necessary, but available funds are still limited. For years, the spending power of the UNEP Environment Fund amounted to only $30 million. Intergovernmental negotiations in London (June 1990) produced commitments for the ozone layer conservation fund to a total of $120 million. Given the extent of overdue reconstruction requirements such fund proportions are still less than modest.[8] The distribution of fund contributions is a politically very sensible issue. With respect to transnational pollution processes few people will deny that the industrialised countries of the OECD will have to bear the largest part of the financial burden. Given their historical share in pollution processes and their current share in consumption of natural resources this is hardly deniable.[9] However, when it comes to concrete commitments, large industrialised countries fail to face their responsibility (for example, the USA in the case of CO_2 emissions). When measured by the number of international conferences on environmental issues during the last couple of years, awareness of the need for action against global environmental degradation is manifestly increasing. Minor 'repair funds' and conscience-raising inter-governmental conferences, of which we have witnessed quite a couple during last years, cannot but only form a first phase of a much more comprehensive restructuring of international economic relations with regard to environmental issues. The World Bank[10] and UNEP finance a range of specific projects and programmes oriented at environmental preservation and reconstruction, but the total amount of funds is still limited. These organisations, in co-operation with NGO's and local governments, can function as more powerful channels for allocation of reparation funds to developing regions, if their financial means and their mandate are strengthened.

The second discussion element concerns how future growth patterns should look like, if they are in order to minimise ongoing environmental damage and natural resource depletion in commodity-producing nations. There is relatively broad agreement in the literature [*Turner, 1988; UNCTAD, 1990c; ECE, 1990*] that four categories of adjustment are required to obtain sustainable patterns of development:

(1) development and introduction of production techniques and policy instruments that reduce pollution output;
(2) development and introduction of techniques oriented at recycling waste products and non-renewable resources;
(3) minimising total use of non-renewable resources by shifting towards renewable resources (provided that the regenerative capacity of renewable resources is maintained), with the proper rate of exploitation of non-renewable resources being related to the availability of alternative investment opportunities;[11]
(4) reduction of pollutive and natural resource-intensive consumption patterns.

World-wide implementation of such adjustments, especially (3) and (4), is unlikely due to a wide divergence of interests. Developing countries do not have the same priority ranking as industrialised countries have. Their most important policy target is to raise the level of per capita income and economic growth. For them pressures to curb consumption (4) – other than for foreign exchange constraints and growth constraints – form a non-item, unless this were coupled with global redistribution of purchasing power. A similar disagreement arises around adjustment category (3). For their economic growth they need investments in (often imported) equipment, technology and intermediates, which make export earnings vital. In so far as reduction of natural resource use implies a reduction of export opportunities for their commodities, this will at least be received with mixed feelings, unless foregone export earnings are fully compensated in another way. Similar disagreement will arise with regard to adjustment category (1). Because of fierce competition in overcrowded international commodity markets a constant pressure on commodity prices exists, translating itself in pressure on production costs. To the extent that alternative, environment-friendly production techniques and related policies conflicts with the need to lower production costs, their introduction will be severely hampered. Unless, again, they are compensated for additional costs.

THE 'NON-POLLUTER GETS PAID' PRINCIPLE

From these observations it can be derived that to arrive internationally at a different, sustainable growth model, adoption of the following guidelines is required for Third World commodity exporters:

* developing countries need further growth of income and consumption per capita;
* to the extent that retrenchment of natural resource use leads to reduction of Third World commodity exports, the latter countries should be monetarily compensated for lost earnings and for the costs of diversifying their export basis;
* incremental production costs incurred by commodity associated exporters with the introduction of ecologically closer-to-optimal production techniques or additional measures for environment protection should be subsidised.[12]

Implementing these guidelines, which represent the 'Non-Polluter Gets Paid' (NPGP) principle, should be tied to a transitional period. Given the wide dispersion of income levels among countries, the period could be fairly long for some primary commodity-dependent countries. Moreover, implementation of the NPGP principle should be shaped in such a form that it doesn't destroy the incentive for the country (and its producers) to change their export base in an ecologically closer-to-optimal way.

Basically, the principle has two components: an adjustment component, and a financing and redistribution component. When OECD countries (and possibly some OPEC countries and NIC's) would consider it purely as a financing instrument, their contribution would be considered as a voluntary addition to their development aid. The supplement could take the form of balance of payment support, project aid and/or technical assistance. Future proportions of the contribution would be exposed to the same budgetary arbitrariness as other national development aid budgets, even if funds are channelled via multilateral organisations. They would remain a gift rather than representing a contractual obligation to pay the full price in a trade transaction. Commodity markets would continue to function in such a way that prices do not reflect the full social cost of production, and that OECD consumers gratuitously reap a part of producing countries' welfare. Technological and organisational innovation would continue to receive wrong price incentives. Environmentally undesirable consumption patterns would persist because prices did not reflect real costs.[13] The economic signal system emits misleading hints.

INTERNALISING ENVIRONMENTAL EXTERNALITIES

Adjustments necessary for sustainable development can be brought about by regulating output or inputs, supplemented by creating monitoring and policing institutions. It would introduce many aspects of a command economy with all its rigidities, efficiency losses, and disincentives for technological innovation. If, however, the capitalist market economy is to remain the dominant allocation system, as seems to be the political spirit of the age, then policies for sustainable development must be concerned about internalising environmental externalities. Adjustments will have to be brought about by price incentives from markets, either on the cost side or on the revenue side. Commodities produced by ecologically more sound techniques must either fetch a price premium or bring a cost advantage. Economic theory offers two main approaches for internalising environmental externalities. Both are based on the 'Polluter Pays' principle.

The first method is associated with Pigou's [1920] proposal to impose 'corrective' taxes so that private agents incorporate in their decisions the effect of their actions on others. Application of this remedy is not very promising with regard to Third World commodity exports. A pivotal condition – the existence of a robustly operating government and tax system – is not satisfied, because of the multiplicity of governments and tax systems. A second problem is that some form of transfer to the *damaged* parties will be needed in order to prevent an undesired lowering of total output by individual action of the producing agents [*Pezzey, 1988: 204–5*]. Furthermore, who are to be regarded as damaged parties, given the fact that it is the structure of international commodity trade that prevents Third World producers from demanding a price that reflects the full social cost. In the short term industries and consumers in importing nations are beneficiaries of transferred welfare from producing countries, so that the latter (that is, the *'polluters'*) are to be compensated.[14] Pigovian taxes will not end the environmental externality when producers take the tax costs for their own account. Whether this happens or not depends on market form and costs of alternative techniques. This hints at a final problem, the question at what level corrective taxes should be fixed so that the undesired externality will be halted. Brown Weiss [1988] pleads for instituting international tolls on the use of common resources like seas, oceans, and air. The proportions of this toll are somewhat arbitrary, and the connection between pollution creation and the costs of environmental protection is only indirectly established. In Brown Weiss's proposal the revenues are to be used for financing clean energies and monitoring agencies.

A second cluster of approaches towards internalisation of externalities is mostly associated with an article of Coase [1960]. His proposition, labeled by others as Coase's theorem, is that bargaining among agents over allowable levels of externalities achieves efficiency without detailed intervention of a central government. To attain that situation a government should take two steps. It has in some way or another to privatise the rights to use its amenities,[15] thereby ending its public good character. Also, it has to guarantee that negotiation about exploitation of these rights is costless, so that it does not involve transaction costs for any party.

The Coasian approach may be useful in some ways to alleviate the 'tragedy of the commons'. For our aim it does not seem appropriate, however, since it presupposes a national government that takes care for legal entitlements and liability rules for individual producers [Berge, 1990]. In the world market there is no such supranational authority and generally accepted legal order. Neither property rights for (use of) the environment nor the claimant status of damaged parties are internationally acknowledged. Even if they were, the second step (eliminating transaction costs for individual negotiations) could turn out to be very expensive. Widely diverging bargaining power positions in international commodity markets would have to be smoothed.[16] Finally, Coase's approach has been criticised because it presupposes that bargaining parties take a long-term view and are not chasing short-term gains [Cooter, 1989].

For our purpose the main flaw of both traditional approaches is their basis in an idea of sovereign nation-states and the basic presupposition of a central (government) authority that is able to function as a unity. Internationally this precondition does not apply. In the sphere of regulations on specific topics the function of an integrative central authority could be reached by intergovernmental agreements and covenants. As long as the United Nations do not have a supranational status, international treaties and covenants are the only possible way. Some progress has been made among industrialised OECD countries and European Community members, for example, national fishing quotas, national quotas for chlorofluorocarbon (CFC) emissions. In OECD countries a large number of environmental policy instruments associated with the 'Polluter Pays' principle are being developed [*Opschoor and Vos, 1989*]. Internationally, such instruments are non-existent so far. A main stumbling block for international treaties that apply the 'Polluter Pays' principle is probably the distribution of income among nations. Problems occur when they are to be extended to countries at very different levels of development and with different priorities with respect to environment and protection of natural resources [*Opschoor, 1990*]. In this situation it seems more promising to endeavour to conclude international treaties incorporating the 'Non-Polluter Gets Paid' principle.

With regard to primary commodities, international treaties regulating this trade do not have to start from scratch. A tradition of toughly negotiated international commodity agreements exists. An important characteristic of those agreements is that they established links between production, consumption, and trade conditions of specific primary commodities. The rest of this article will be devoted to possibilities for internalising of environmental externalities in international commodity prices by similar international agreements.

ENVIRONMENTAL PREMIUM

Although powerful ecology movements hardly exist in most Third World countries, their governments are more and more aware of the need to minimise damage to the environmental resource base that supports their commodity exports. Given the need to continue the flow of export earnings, better environmental care will have to come primarily from the use of ecologically nearer-to-optimal production techniques that have already been developed elsewhere. In agricultural and forestry technology increasing attention has been given to the development of non-chemical forms of pest management (integrated pest management), 'green' fertilisers to replace (most) chemical fertilisers, harvest rotation, use of low-input varieties, mulching, integration of agriculture and forestry (agro-forestry), and systematic reafforestation. In hilly areas economic self-interest and ecology can be combined by helping farmers shift from grain to tree crops by providing them with advice, equipment, and marketing assistance [*Ghatak, 1988; Pearce et al., 1990*]. Sometimes it will be necessary to supplement commodity production with additional production to neutralise harmful effects, like sewerage systems, water cleaning and other forms of waste clearance, anti-erosion dikes and other sedimentation techniques. Irrigation techniques can often be optimised so that better use is made of available water resources [*Barbier, 1990*].

In mining, especially in developed countries with stiffer ecological norms, exploitation techniques have been developed and applied that do less harm to the environment: construction of waste water reservoirs; air and water cleaning; refilling of open-pit mines; various forms of erosion abatement, like storage and reconstruction of removed top soils; systematic reafforestation.

Existence and feasibility of alternative techniques can only be established on a commodity-by-commodity basis, often with necessary region-specific modifications. This being done, it is possible to establish how alternative production techniques influence initial investment and operating costs, relative to current techniques.[17] More probable than not, such alternatives will demonstrate to be more expensive, because additional cost elements are included while not being matched by a proportional increase in productivity. A price premium for commodities produced in this way is required to cover extra costs, specifically for the recurrent element of extra costs. For brevity's sake this price premium will be labelled *environmental premium*. A practical form of internalisation of externalities would be to get this premium included in the commodity's world market price.

When it comes to application of an environmental premium, the question arises whether it should be a generic or a differentiated mark-up on the 'free market' commodity price. A differentiated level could reflect different rates of cost increase in various producing countries, but it would at the same time introduce redistributive elements. In order to keep interference with market prices as limited as possible a differentiated level is less desirable. Besides, it would require additional administration and bureaucracy. A generic level of the environmental premium, with the same nominal proportions for all countries, is preferable, therefore. It has to be recognised that, for two reasons, a generic premium level works out differently for various producing countries. First, there will be differences in ecological side effects of production in various countries. In some countries a generic premium will not completely compensate all incremental costs of abatement of pollution and other undesired side effects of commodity production. At the same time, a generic price increase will in some countries overcompensate such cost increments, thus contributing to a higher average profit margin for these exporters. This differential effect reflects comparative ecological advantages.[18] These cannot be expected to correlate in a systematic way with production scale. Yet in a second way a generic environmental premium on the world market price does work out differently for various exporting countries. This is a consequence of economies of scale in pollution abatement. To the extent that alternative technologies are characterised by indivisibilities and cause discrete additions to fixed investment requirements, large-scale producers enjoy the advantage of sinking fixed unit costs. This is illustrated by Figures 1 and 2 on the basis of a random numerical example.

FIGURE 1

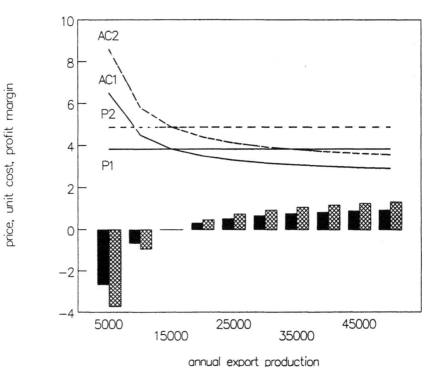

annual export production

In Figure 1 the magnitude of the environmental premium is fixed in such a way that the relation between average unit costs (AC1, AC2) and world market price (P1, P2) is left unaltered for the marginal producers, that is, those exporting 15,000 units per year. The black bars (old situation) and crosshatched bars (new situation) indicate unit profit margins, and show economies of scale in pollution abatement. In Figure 2 the level is determined by the principle that the profit margin for the 'average' producers (say, those producing 25,000 units annually) should be left unaltered. The unit price in the second case is slightly lower thus causing some marginal producers to drop out.

FIGURE 2

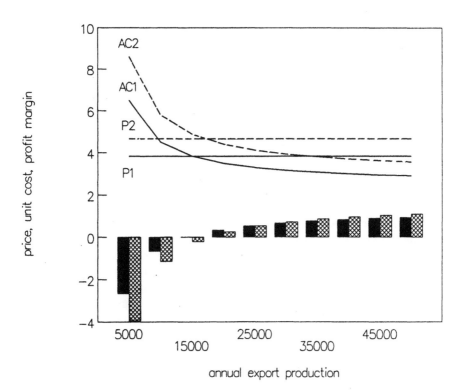

annual export production

INTERNATIONAL ENVIRONMENT AND COMMODITY AGREEMENTS

In a situation where many debt-ridden Third World countries compete
with each other in the same commodities and try to increase their export
volumes, it will be hard to realise the environmental premium. International
trading houses, manufacturing firms, and other importers in developed
countries skilfully play the 'Divide et Impera'-game, thus contributing to
the same effect. The free market solution seems to offer meagre prospects.
International arrangements and market regulation form a prerequisite for
internalisation of the environmental premium.

International commodity agreements belong to the scarce institutional
forms for regulation of international markets. For some commodities
(wheat, tin) international arrangements were already in function before
the Second World War, though most of them stem from the 1970s. Usually
two types of these intergovernmental agreements are discerned: those with,
and those without economic mechanisms (like manipulatable bufferstocks
and quota systems). The former are called *formal* agreements and aim at

stabilising the world market price of the commodity. Moreover, and this they have in common with *informal* agreements, they specify guidelines for exchange of (statistical) information on production, trade flows and consumption of the commodity, and for promotion of new commodity applications.

At the 1976 Nairobi UNCTAD conference some agreement was reached on an Integrated Programme on Commodities (IPC) that should (1) improve the position of Third World commodity producers and, at the same time, (2) stabilise commodity prices. It would contain an $11 billion common fund to finance buffer stocks to support – by an equal number of formal commodity agreements – the prices of some 19 primary commodities. Later on this was reduced to ten 'core' commodities. The atmosphere in which the original agreement was reached, was certainly influenced by the successful actions of OPEC and high prices for many other commodities. OECD countries were most interested in the second objective. From a theoretic angle the potential dissonance between both objectives was pointed out in an early phase.[19] As time went on disagreement increased on the relative weight of both objectives. When, with a time lag of ten years, the common fund became ratified by the required minimum number of countries and received the required minimal amount of pledges for funds, its proportions had been drastically reduced (to about $0.5 billion). Formal agreements were concluded for sugar, coffee, natural rubber, cocoa and tin. Most of them have been discontinued since then. Disagreement between producing countries and/or non-participation of important consumer countries led to the disintegration of the cocoa and coffee agreements. In 1991 the only remaining effective formal agreement is the International Natural Rubber Agreement.

The collapse of the International Tin Agreement in October 1985 revealed painfully that it is impossible to maintain a stable reference price at a high level against secular market trends. The financial burden of increasing bufferstock proportions increases beyond the level that not only consumption countries but also producing countries are prepared to carry. The last agreements for cocoa and rubber both included a mechanism for periodic adjustment of the reference price to 'free' market prices. Falling commodity prices[20] and subsequent balance of payment problems of many producing countries during the 1980s placed the need for stabilisation of export earnings again on the international agenda. Rather than returning to the original commodity agreements, there is increasing support for the vision that stabilisation of *export earnings* is better served by international compensation arrangements. Examples exist in the form of the IMF Compensatory and Contingency Financing Facility and the Stabex arrangement of the Lomé Treaty. Both offer financial compensation for loss of export earnings due to commodity pricefluctuations.

In spite of their decreasing international popularity it must be recognised that international commodity agreements belong to the very scarce international institutions capable of establishing direct links between consumption, trade and production. This capacity makes them potentially useful instruments for integration of environmental issues.

Up to now only one commodity agreement, namely the International Tropical Timber Agreement, explicitly includes environmental aspects. In the timber agreement member countries are encouraged 'to support and develop industrial tropical timber reforestation and forest management activities'. Another of its seven objectives is 'to encourage the development of national policies aimed at sustainable utilisation and conservation of tropical forests and their genetic sources, and at maintaining the ecological balance in the regions concerned' [*UNCTAD, 1983: 2*]. For the realisation of these objectives R&D projects in the field of reforestation are promoted, while one of its three subcommittees concerns itself with reafforestation and forest management. The Agreement encourages member countries only on a voluntary basis to promote environmental protection and reforestation. It includes no provisions for directly linking costs of forest reconstruction and timber prices. The need for such instruments is becoming evident, since deforestation continues worldwide with little regard to operational forest management and sustainable timber production [*Poore, 1989*].

Integration of environmental protection elements in such agreements can be extended beyond the terms included in the timber agreement. Intergovernmental negotiations could be used to find agreement on integration in commodity prices of an environmental premium to cover costs of alternative production techniques or environmental reconstruction expenses in producing countries. To distinguish this new type of agreements from earlier experiences we propose to label them *International Environment and Commodity Agreements* (IECAs). A number of preliminary steps are necessary before International Environment and Commodity Agreements (IECAs) can become active. They can be ordered in two phases, a research phase and a negotiation phase.

PRELIMINARY STEPS

During the *research phase* rather detailed technical and economic studies are required relating to ecology, production and functioning of markets for a specific commodity. Five sub-themes can be specified:

(a) Inventarisation and quantification of ecological effects of its export production. Effects will be formulated in terms of several relevant indicators and measures (continuous or discrete) that are relevant for this commodity [e.g. *Nijkamp, 1989; Nash and Bowers, 1988*].

(b) Assessment of relevant alternative production techniques and additional measures that would limit the most important negative environmental effects, with an indication (on purely technical criteria) of a time path for implementation.

(c) Appraisal of economic effects of alternative production techniques and additional measures, with regard to production costs and production volumes. This has to include a tentative assessment of effects on import requirements, employment and production regions. For the best alternative techniques the incremental cost price relative to costs under current techniques has to be established, thus indicating the magnitude of the gross price mark-up that will be necessary. Incremental cost effects in some important export countries must be estimated.

(d) Investigation of probable substitution effects that may occur in consuming countries and industries as a consequences of the estimated gross price mark-up.

(e) Assessment of the optimal form in which the environmental premium is to be institutionalised, that is, import levy or export tax (elaborated in a later section), and formulation of proposals for procedures, checks, monitoring agencies, and fund management.

For the first four sub-themes it may be necessary to differentiate between the main producing countries. The study on fourth sub-theme should specifically pay attention to the reaction of all relevant economic agents. From the point of view of consumers the price mark-up, in whichever form it is levied, functions as a turnover tax on the international price of the commodity. Because of the small part of commodity prices in the costs of most final products, substitution effects on the consumer side tend to be small. Most substitution effects may be expected from manufacturing agents and large importers. How price elasticity affects their demand for the commodity has to be estimated by considering cross elasticities for viable substitutes.

On the basis of reports on ecological effects (a), technical-economic studies (b, c) and expected market reactions (d) proposals have to be put forward with regard to implementation priorities of alternative techniques and the associated level of the environmental premium. In the fifth sub-study attention it should be considered if and how the Common Fund for Commodities and UNCTAD's IPC programme could facilitate introduction of an International Environment and Commodity Agreement.

NEGOTIATION ISSUES

The *negotiation phase* builds upon the results and proposals of the first phase. Most probably, the studies will contain a number of variants rather than clear-cut, unambiguous conclusions on the issues involved. Across various diverging interests – between producing and consuming nations, between producing countries with different production conditions, between ecological action groups, governments, and established interests in commodity chains (like transnational companies) – agreement has to be reached on a number of issues. The most important of them are:

Decision criterion for determining the magnitude of the environmental premium. If a generic premium level is preferred, it has to be decided which reference countries will be used for determining the increase in average units costs due to alternative techniques, and the required price mark-up. Should the premium level be such that marginal producers are kept in the market or should 'average' producers be taken as benchmark.

Levels of unacceptable ecological damage. Which types and levels (for all relevant criteria) of negative environmental externalities should be abated? Discussion can be expected on policy-induced versus 'average technology'-induced ecological damage (elaborated in a following section).

Magnitude of the environmental premium. Having established the reference countries, the ecological effects that have to be neutralised, and the incremental costs (given known technologies), it is possible to fix the level of the environmental premium. Some other considerations may enter the discussion, however. For producing nations a trade-off exists between ecological damage and the potential loss of export earnings which is likely given a certain price elasticity of commodity demand. Their attitude depends among other things on the availability of export diversification alternatives. For consuming nations a trade-off exists between current cheap commodity supply versus tolerating further ecological damage in producing countries that bolsters future threats to the global ecosystem. It is to be expected that their tolerance levels will be lower in cases where immediate health damage may be caused in consuming nations, for example, due to pesticide residues in agricultural commodities.

Indicator of reference price. If the level of the environmental premium is fixed on the basis of average price-cost margins in the situation before introduction of alternative techniques, then it has to be decided which price indicator will serve as reference price. One could use an existing, internationally used price indicator at certain agreed point in time or a weighted international price trend that is calculated in an agreed way. Also the frequency of adjustment to new reference price levels has to be decided upon.

Finally, governments must achieve an agreement on a number of questions relating to the *institutional form* in which the price mark-up will be introduced (import surcharge, export tax or other forms). Associated with this conclusion are decisions on *monitoring system, government representation, and sanction procedures* to guarantee that the price premium will be paid and that resulting extra earnings will be allocated to expenses for environmental reconstruction and conservation as agreed upon in the agreement. Finally, some dynamic procedures[21] must be endorsed.

The negotiation process draws heavily on a well-understood long-term self-interest of nations. The most important divergences of opinion will probably spring from short-term interests and regional or country-group egoism. An essential negotiation element will be how to cope with *free-riders*. If countries systematically share the benefits of an International Environment and Commodity Agreement (IECA) without carrying part of its burden, this forms a time bomb under the agreement. Free-ridership can occur both between countries and within countries. Handling this problem will be a important determinant in the choice of the eventual institutional form of the IECA.

IMPORT LEVY AND OTHER IMPLEMENTATION ALTERNATIVES

The environmental price mark-up can be levied in several forms, each having its own advantages and disadvantages. Because it is a premium on top of a 'given' world market price, and because it regards a form of international redistribution, it seems obvious to charge this levy when commodities pass a border. This may be the border of the exporting country or that of the (ultimate) importing country. In the first case it has the form of an export tax, in the latter case it is an import toll.

The *export tax variant* has two less attractive implications. One implication is that commodity-importing Third World countries will also face a higher import bill. If the international community agrees on the principle that most of the financial burden of the environmental reconstruction and conservation will have to be borne by the OECD countries, additional measures have to be taken. The most direct way to elaborate this principle could be a compensatory fund.[22] Secondly, guarantees have to be created against free-riding by exporting countries. Free-riding behaviour can occur by either not levying the export tax (to secure extra market share) or by using the revenues for other purposes. Since these funds are fungible, it is tempting to simply add them to general profits of the exporting companies, or to general public revenues. To prevent such forms of free riding the IECA Secretariat (or an auditing committee of it) should have the right to inspect:

(a) *exporting companies*, to check whether the price mark-up is actually charged by the exporter and whether these revenues were reserved and used for the right purposes. Moreover, the origin of exported commodities has to be verified, in order to prevent misuse by re-export or blending of commodities from countries where no export tax is levied.

(b) financial transactions of producing countries' *national governments* related to the export tax. The auditing task would be facilitated by creation of a special account or administrative body for transfer of funds from the price mark-up.

(c) *production locations*, to verify whether ecologically more sound production techniques and processes are being implemented.

The inspection committee or IECA secretariat would report any irregularity and would formulate proposals for corrective steps to the government of the exporting country. Some arbitration and sanction rules will be required. If a government and the IECA do not reach agreement a problem arises.[23] A preliminary conclusion may be that implementation in the form of export taxes is marred by additional measures and international bureaucracy. Auditing procedures may easily interfere with national sovereignty feelings of producing countries.

None of these problems arise with the *import levy variant*. Charging the environmental premium at the border of importing countries makes it possible to charge only OECD countries, and perhaps some NICs and OPEC countries. The import surcharge should be commodity-specific and will have to be paid by importers in commodity-importing developed countries. They pay a fixed amount per quantity imported to the fiscal authorities of their national government.[24] By levying on a generic basis on all imported quantities, the need to check for origins (due to re-export) is eliminated. It also thwarts the incentive for free-ridership on the side of exporting countries. Governments of importing countries periodically transfer the revenues from the surcharge to a special environment fund, administered by the IECA board. Exporting countries and a statistical department of the IECA secretariat together assess annual total export volume and its country destinations. On basis of this, with a correction for re-exports, the gross payable amount for each importing country is easily assessed. Free-riding by importing countries will be difficult. Governments of producing countries can make drawings from environment fund, with maximal drawing rights proportional to their export volume. Definitive remittance of allotted funds is dependent upon the content and soundness of the proposals put forward by governments. The financing proposals formulated by governments (perhaps on behalf of exporting companies in their country) concern specific projects for additional investments in ecology-friendly production methods, subsidy programmes for use of alternative production methods or inputs,[25] and local environmental preservation projects in commodity-producing areas. The IECA could offer technical, organisational and economical assistance to governments to help them formulating feasible proposals for funding. Evaluation of project proposals by the IECA could be based on: expected ecological effect, technical and organisational feasibility, effectiveness of earlier fund disbursements to the country.[26]

In current economic practice initiatives for creation of import levies for environmental purposes have seen their debut. It regards the European timber trade organisations, which are under growing public pressure to limit import of tropical hardwoods. Timber traders are themselves becoming increasingly aware of the fact that future tropical timber sources have become insecure, as countries like the Philippines have already abandoned timber exports [*Blackwell, 1991*]. Now organisations of timber importers in several European countries (for example, United Kingdom, Netherlands) are becoming aligned with some environment conservation groups in lobbying their governments for a surcharge *on the import prices* of tropical hardwood. This surcharge (extra import levy) will be used to fund – through the International Tropical Timber Organisation – the development of sustainable tropical timber resources. If such a system comes into existence exporting countries can make drawings from this fund for reafforestation projects.

Compared to the one based on export taxes the import levy variant has as relative disadvantage that the connection between commodity export production and implementation of environment-preserving techniques becomes less direct. Internalisation of environmental externalities in world commodity prices is accomplished in an indirect way. This relative disadvantage is, however, more than compensated by being relatively easily applicable and by limiting possibilities for free-riding.

Success of International Environment and Commodity Agreements (IECAs) will partly depend on some product and market characteristics. The commodity must have a certain degree of homogeneity regarding quality and variety. The main producing and consuming nations must participate in the agreement, so that market transactions outside the sphere of the IECA can be limited in magnitude and number. Stable supply conditions must prevail, so as to avoid sharp discrepancies between (a) the interests of traditional producers and newcomers, and (b) sharply diverging production costs in the different producing countries. The demand side of the international market should have some stability. Dominating market positions of large trading houses or commodity speculators that benefit from the continuation of highly volatile prices are an unfavourable factor. Strong volatility of prices creates extra problems for assessing levels and total amounts of environmental price levies. In cases where supply and demand side of the commodity market are dominated by one or a small number of transnational corporations regulating a large part of international transactions on an intracompany or semi-intracompany base (that is, by vertical integration or long-term supply contracts) some extra audit measures by the IECA board will be required. This situation would not necessarily constrain success, provided that a comparison is possible with an accepted international arm's length price, and provided that involved governments have adequate statistical or customs services for monitoring their international trade, so that the freedom to manipulate intracompany prices is limited.

DEPLETABLE RESOURCES AND POLICY-INDUCED EXTERNALITIES

The IECA model which has been described so far, only takes into account *current* costs for environmental protection and reconstruction. It does not offer a solution for depletion of non-renewable resources, though this issue is important in the cases of tropical timber[27] and mining products. Non-renewables have intentionally been left out of consideration for both theoretical and practical reasons. Assessment of the optimal depletion path implies a number of highly disputable valuation questions. One concerns intergenerational equity: how should the time preference of current consumers be evaluated against the demands of all future generations? How should the latter be discounted? In which way will future generations deal with the skewed historic-geographical distribution of the consumption of depletable natural resources? What are the current value implications of future technical innovations in recycling, material-saving and the use of non-scarce natural substitutes? Even without these issues accomplishment of IECAs will put a strain on international willingness to compromise, and on the long-term vision of national governments in producing and importing countries. In order to avoid a paralysing international dispute on these matters, it seems preferable to make a start with a price mark-up that allows current suboptimal techniques to be discarded or minimised in the production of primary commodities in developing countries. If experience with IECAs is satisfying, an atmosphere may be created in which it is possible to reach international agreement on price mark-ups or other instruments that explicitly deal with economic valuation of non-renewable resources.

Apart from the non-renewables issue, discussion on IECAs will be complicated by simultaneous existence of negative ecological externalities caused by market failure (public goods, absence of negative prices for pollution products) and those caused by wrong policy. International Environment and Commodity Agreements are set primarily for the first type of externalities and do not offer a solution for the second type. This is not to say, however, that the second type of externalities is not important in relation to the production of primary export commodities. In many developing countries degradation of environmental quality is encouraged by and even subsided by local governments, some times in co-operation with foreign donors and companies [*Le Prestre, 1989: 170; Pearce et al., 1990; Gillis and Repetto, 1987*].

The role of governments can differ very much between one commodity and another. Two poles can be discerned, between which a large number of mixed cases exists. On the one hand we find commodities of which production is based on concessions given out by governments. This is often found in mining and forestry. Government policies that regard deforestation or mining development primarily as economic extension projects, and accordingly subsidise them, without much regard to ecological aspects, cause negative environmental externalities of a policy-induced nature. Large infrastructural projects by governments often explicitly aim at opening up natural landscapes and rain forests for concession areas. For instance, in Gabon and Brazil this has contributed to ecological degradation of rain forests. Allotment of short-term concession encourages short-term behaviour, sub-maintainance of the concession base, and neglect of lagged ecological consequences. In the case of concession-based commodity production governments have powerful and rather direct tools for compelling allottees to observe certain ecological conditions for exploitation. In Malaysia, for instance, the government introduced a hallmark for export timber, ensuring that concessionaires produced it by sustainable forestry methods. Ecological degradation of concession areas could be reduced by stricter control of concessionaires and prohibitive financial penalties in case of harmful exploitation.

At the other extreme we find commodities predominantly produced by small, decentrally operating small producers, as is often the case with coffee and cocoa. Governmental grip on this type of commodity production is much more indirect, yet not absent. Via extension services, marketing boards, pricing policy, subsidies for fertilisers, pesticides and high yielding varieties of seed, and rural credit policy government already influences production conditions. This set of instruments – incentives and disincentives – can also be used to foster ecological preservation. Existing commodity purchasing channels (exporters and local merchants) can get a useful complementary role once they can be persuaded to include ecological quality standards in their overall quality monitoring.[28] Increasing the availability of rural credit at affordable rates and terms could relieve ecological strain and allow proper investments in conservation, particularly for marginal farmers, that now often overexploit their soils and environment due to lack of (income) alternatives. Extension services could play an important role in dissemination of ecologically more appropriate techniques (for example, integrated pest management, ploughing techniques) and more appropriate varieties. There is a role for governments in developing local agronomic research on more appropriate production techniques.

An important consequence of growing international attention for environmental problems is probably that unwanted and unanticipated ecological effects of government policies in developing countries will be reduced in the future. The World Bank 'ecologised' its policy since 1987 and now supports transfer of sustainable production technologies to Third World governments. Given this change in awareness it can be expected that, internationally, the accent will shift more and more to environmental externalities that are caused by market failure, rather than wrong government policies.

CONCLUSION

Damage to the ecosystem in developing countries is often related to production of primary export commodities. Education and conscience-raising programmes may increase awareness of side effects of production activities. But it will not necessarily stop negative environmental externalities associated with export production. Government policies for raising export income may even increase such effects, because environmental concern tends not to be put in the first place of their priority rankings. Economic growth and poverty abatement objectives are generally considered far more important, although ecological concern is manifestly increasing in most developing countries. Economic growth requires investments and imports, for which foreign exchange earnings by primary commodities exports are vital in many developing countries. Given this need for a continuing flow of export earnings, introduction of more ecology-friendly production techniques will only be possible if producers would be compensated for the extra costs of such techniques. This would require the adoption of the 'Non-Polluter Gets Paid' (NPGP) principle in international commodity trade between commodity-exporting developing countries and industrialised countries. Growing awareness of transnational threats to the global ecosystem increases the latter countries' willingness-to-pay for environmental preservation in vital areas like conservation of the world's stock of rain forests. Therefore, a climate is coming into existence in which adoption of the NPGP principle is becoming feasible. In international negotiations on ozone layer depletion and global warming effect this principle is on the brink of being adopted.

Apart from a generic application of the principle, for example, in the form of a Climate Fund or a separate fund to help less developed countries ban CFC-gasses, it can also be used to integrate environmental externalities in prices of primary export commodities. Commodity prices do not reflect real costs of environmental destruction, which is to a large extent due to market failure. In this article it is argued that the NPGP principle could very well materialise in the creation of International Environment and Commodity Agreements (IECAs). Such agreements would incorporate procedures and institutions for putting an environmental premium on top of existing commodity prices. This ecological mark-up would primarily be used to finance alternatives techniques and measures that allow environmental conservation and reconstruction in commodity producing areas. The most appropriate form for levying the environmental premium is probably that of an import surcharge in importing countries, but introduction of an IECA will require additional research for each specific commodity. Successful application of the NPGP principle in International Environment and Commodity Agreements will function as an example for a wider approach to integrate environmental externalities in world market prices.

NOTES

1. 'If Africa's economies are to grow, they must earn foreign exchange to pay for essential imports. Thus it is vital that they increase their share of world markets. The prospects for most primary commodities are poor, so higher export earnings must come from increased output, diversification into new commodities and an aggressive export drive into the rapidly growing Asian markets' [*World Bank, 1989: 13*]. In the light of recent historical experience these World Bank proposals seem questionable [*Kox, 1990*].
2. In 1988 primary commodities (including oil) accounted for more than half of total exports in 108 developing countries. In 88 countries the dependency percentage amounted even to more than 70 per cent of total exports [*UNCTAD, 1990a*].
3. Export production is not always the only reason for deforestation. In some countries

(for example, Brazil) deforestation is also caused by a skewed division of land or by a government policy (for example, Indonesia) favouring agricultural extension in remote forest regions by domestic settlers.

4. For example, there have already been a number of unexpected ecological collapses in economically important fisheries [WRI and IIED, 1986; NAS, 1986].

5. Because of its basically microeconomic character the method is also used for locational decisions of transnational companies [UNCTC, 1985].

6. It does not count costs of a decreased protection function of the forest (watershed protection, maintainance of a micro climate, biodiversity) and lower potential tourism income [Barbier, 1990].

7. Large population pressure in a region with limited ecological carrying capacity causes similar effects. Disintegration of social structures that ensured maintainance of common grounds, also contributed to overgrazing and erosion.

8. Ettinger et al. [1990: 21–4] estimate the required total annual investment costs for dealing with the greenhouse problem at $330 billion (of which $100 billion to be spent in developing countries) while an additional Climate Fund of $25 billion would be necessary to alleviate developing countries' current financial burden which would stem from such investments. The minimal dimension of an emergency facility of the Climate Fund is estimated to amount to $1 billion. Wicke and Hucke [1989: 292–304] estimate total annual costs for an 'Ecological Marshall Plan' at $190 billion in 1993, increasing to $651 billion in 2013.

9. In the case of world consumption of commercial energy 70 per cent is annually consumed by only one-fifth of the world's population [WCED, 1987].

10. After much criticism of its support for ecologically harmful programmes as the Polonoroeste programme (in the Brazilian Amazone region) and the Indonesian transmigration program the World Bank reoriented its lending policy in 1987 [Le Prestre, 1989]. Since then it explicitly announced a 'greening' of its projects [Finance & Development, Feb. 1990].

11. Biophysical economists (for example, Georgescu-Roegen, Costanza, Daly, Cleveland) consider this category of adjustments as too optimistic and partial a solution for resource depletion and increasing entropy levels [Cleveland, 1987; Daly, 1989].

12. In the case of reducing chlorofluorocarbons (CFCs) emissions, harmful for the ozone layer, this principle has already been accepted in intergovernmental negotiations.

13. Galtung's [1990] proposes to shorten pollution chains for consumers, so that these chains become more visible and tangible. He illustrates this by a provoking, but clarifying proposal to make it obligatory that exhaust pipes of cars end inside the car instead of outside. The motivation to buy only clean cars would be greatly enhanced!

14. Echoing Keynes ('In the long run we all are dead') national boundaries become irrelevant in the long term, because both country categories lose from environmental destruction.

15. This could be done by pollution taxes, by auction of pollution permits, and by distributing licenses that specify a a maximal pollution emission per company [Siebert, 1987: 91–8; Pezzey, 1988].

16. The 'Coase theorem' states that the allocative result of negotiations will be independent from the initial distribution of property rights. It has been criticised because the negotiation result is not independent from income distribution between parties. It is evident that between trading agents in a given commodity chain wide differences in negotiation power can coexist, for example, between large transnational trading companies, local governments or marketing boards, and small farmers. Correction of these differences by a government can be expected to be expensive. Moreover, there is no intrinsic reason to limit the set of parties that are damaged by externalities, to only production units. A similar status could be claimed, for example, for forest inhabitants whose existence and territory is distressed by timber production.

17. A range of alternatives may have to be considered. A study of a large number of Canadian mining sites for non-ferrous metals over the period 1951–74 evaluated the economic effects of water pollution control for 'standard' and 'best-possible' techniques. Pollution control measures necessary under the prevailing governmental regulations amounted to

three to ten per cent of total mine investment and 2–5 per cent of operating costs. However, if the best possible water treatment schemes (given known technology) would be employed, the figures would rise to 13 per cent of total investment and eight per cent of operating costs [*Blunden, 1985: 53*].

18. Differential effects on profit margin tends to stimulate production in countries with a comparative ecological advantage, and thus invokes a change in international supply conditions of the commodity. On the other hand, the eventual form of the IECA should be such that it does not form an incentive for exporters with a relative disadvantage to dismiss cost-increasing pollution abatement and other environment preservation measures.

19. Only under special conditions will measures for price stabilisation simultaneously increase or stabilise incomes of producers in developing countries. 'Our main conclusion is that price stabilisation schemes have limited efficacy in stabilising the real spendable income of producing countries and that most of the other benefits associated with the stabilisation schemes are transfer benefits which, in many cases, seem to benefit the consuming countries at the expense of the producing countries' [*Newbery and Stiglitz, 1981: 39–40*].

20. In 1989 the average real price of non-fuel commodities from developing countries was only 78 per cent of its 1980 level [*IMF, 1990: 27*].

21. The magnitude of the price markup is determined by several variables of a dynamic nature: technical innovation (feasible alternative production methods), changes in the international reference price, and price developments of commodity substitutes. As part of a monitoring system a subcommittee of the International Environment and Commodity Agreements may be charged with a permanent review of ecological, technological, and economic conditions in the commodity branch. The subcommittee could periodically present proposals on necessary adjustments of the price mark-up.

22. The fund could be fed by direct contributions of OECD members and more developed NICs, or by transfer of part of export tax revenue from the exporting countries. Contributions could be proportional to either their exports or imports of the commodity. Management, proportions, and drawing right are to be settled separately.

23. Juridical enforcement of IECA rules is only possible by a litigation in a court in the country with which a dispute exists. Internationally, only arbitrage (for example, for the International Court of Justice in The Hague) can be hoped for [cf. *Stein and Grenville-Wood, 1985*]. However, juridical enforcement seems not the most appropriate way to regulate an escalated major conflict, as actual economic functioning of the IECA in many cases will be enfeebled before a settlement is reached.

24. Customs clearance in the port of entry should be the determining criterion. It avoids troubles with differences between physical and non-physical (futures) trade.

25. In case of commodities where production is dominated by small-scale producers, governments need programmes that offer subsidies for implementation for specific production methods and inputs. In the implementation of such programmes land extension services or local authorities can play a role. To the extent that production methods and or input use during production can be diagnosed in the product itself (for example, chemical residues) commercial channels in the country (purchasing companies, exporters) can play a useful role in distributing the premium to producers that apply the beneficial production techniques. The ecological properties of the product, possibly in the form of a hall-mark, become a regular quality attribute along with other quality characteristics.

26. Evaluation procedures should be as short as possible, with limited bureaucracy. Use of contracted experts by the IECA secretariat could serve this objective.

27. It is not so certain that tropical timber can be regarded as a renewable resource, like for instance is true in case of most coniferous timber varieties. This incertainty stems from the long growth cycle (40–150 years) for many popular tropical hardwood varieties, the vulnerable ecology of tropical rain forests, and widespread lack of success – except in case of teak – of attempts to regenerate the logged varieties [*Gillis et al., 1987: 522*].

28. This could be facilitated when a government would subsidise distribution of simple and

cheap technical devices for testing of biocide residuals in products. For their support it is crucial that ecologically high quality products fetch a price premium.

REFERENCES

Ahmad, Y.J.(ed.), 1981, 'Evaluating the Environment: Application of Cost-Benefit Analysis to Environmental Protection Measures', UNEP, Nairobi.
Amstel, A. van, Baars, E. Sijm, J. and H. Venne, 1986, 'Tapioca from Thailand for the Dutch Livestock Industry', Occasional Paper R-86/7, Institute for Environmental Studies, Amsterdam.
Barbier, E., 1989, 'Cash Crops, Food Crops, and Sustainability: The Case of Indonesia', *World Development*, 17 (6), pp.879–95.
Barbier, E., 1990, 'Natural Resource Degradation: Policy, Economics and Management', Development Economics Seminar Paper No.90–3/9, ISS, The Hague.
Berge, E., 1990, 'Property Rights Theory as a Basis for Organising Resource Utilisation for a Sustainable Development'. Paper EADI presented at the General conference, Oslo, June 1990.
Bishop, J. and J. Allen, 1989, 'The On-Site Costs of Soil Erosion in Mali', Environment Department Working Paper No.21, World Bank, Washington.
Blackwell, D., 1991, 'New Levels of Awareness – Further Initiatives to Safeguard the World's Rain Forests, in *Financial Times*, special issue on Industry and Environment, 13 March, p.vi.
Blunden, J., 1985, *Mineral Resources and Their Management*, London: Longman.
Brown Weiss, E., 1988, *In Fairness to Future Generations: International Law, Common Patrimony and Intergenerational Equity*, London: Transnational/UNU.
Carlton, D. and G. Loury 1980, 'The Limitations of Pigouvian Taxes as a Long-Run Remedy for Externalities', *Quarterly Journal of Economics*, Vol.95.
Cleveland, C.J., 1987, 'Biophysical Economics: Historical Perspective and Current Research Trends', *Ecological Modelling*, Vol.3 (1/2), Sept., pp.47–73.
Coase, R., 1960, 'The Problem of Social Cost', *Journal of Law and Economics*, Vol.3 (1), Oct., pp.1–44.
Cooter, R.D., 1989, 'The Coase Theorem', in J. Eatwell, M. Milgate and P. Newman, *The New Palgrave: Allocation, Information and Markets*, London: Macmillan.
Daly, H.E., 1989, 'Steady-state and Growth Concepts for the Next Century', in F. Archibugi and P. Nijkamp (eds.), *Economy and Ecology: Towards Sustainable Development*, Dordrecht: Kluwer Academic Publishers, pp.73–87.
Dasgupta, P. and K.-G. Maeler, 1989, 'Social Cost Benefit Analysis and Soil Erosion', in F. Archibugi and P. Nijkamp (eds.), *Economy and Ecology: Towards Sustainable Development*, Dordrecht: Kluwer Academic Publishers, pp.221–60.
ECE, 1990, 'Environment and Economics', Document E C.AD/R.49), Secretariat, Economic Commission on Europe, Geneva.
Ettinger, J.van, T. Jansen and C. Jepma, 1990, 'Climate, Environment and Development', Paper presented at the EADI 6th General Conference (27–30 June 1990), Oslo.
Ford Runge, C. and R.M. Nolan, 1990, 'Trade in Disservices; Environmental Regulation and Agricultural Trade', *Food Policy*, Feb. pp.3–8.
Galtung, J. 1990, 'Beyond Brundtland: Linking Global Problems and Local Solution', Paper presented at 6th EADI General Conference on European Development Research, Oslo, June 1990.
Ghatak, S., 1988, 'Towards a Second Green Revolution in the Tropics: From Chemicals to New Biological Techniques for Sustained Economic Development', in R.K. Turner (ed.), *Sustainable Environmental Management: Principles and Practice*, Boulder, CD: Westview Press.
Gilbert, C.L. 1987, 'International Commodity Agreements: Design and Performance', in *World Development*, Vol.15 (5), May.

Gillis, M. and R. Repetto (eds.), 1987, *Public Policy and the Misuse of Resources*, New York: Cambridge University Press.

Goodland R. and G. Ledec, 1987, 'Neoclassical Economics and Principles of Sustainable Development', *Ecological Modelling*, Vol.38 (1/2), Sept., pp.19–46.

Hufschmidt, M. and E. Hyman, 1982, *Economic Approaches to Natural Resource and Environmental Quality Analysis*, Dublin: Tycooly.

IMF, 1990, 'Primary Commodities – Market Developments and Outlook', Commodities Division of the Research Department, International Monetary Fund, Washington.

Kox, H., 1990, 'Export Constraints for Sub-Saharan Africa – The Role of Non-Fuel Primary Commodities', Research Memorandum No.1990–91, Economic Faculty, Free University, Amsterdam.

Magrath, W. and P. Arens, 1987, 'The Costs of Soil Erosion on Java – A Natural Resource Accounting Approach', World Resources Institute, Washington.

Mortimore, M., 1989, *Adapting to Drought: Farmers, Famines and Desertification in West Africa*, Cambridge: Cambridge University Press.

Myers, N. and R. Tucker, 1987, 'Deforestation in Central America: Spanish Legacy and North American Consumers', in *Environmental Review*, 11 (1), pp.55–71.

NAS, 1986, *Acid Deposition: Long-Term Trends*, Washington: National Academy Press.

Nash, C. and J. Bowers, 1988, 'Alternative Approaches to the Valuation of Environmental Resources', in R.K. Turner (ed.), *Sustainable Environmental Management: Principles and practice*, Boulder, CO: Westview Press.

Nijkamp, P., 1989, 'Multicriteria Analysis: A Decision Support System for Sustainable Environmental Management', in F. Archibugi and P. Nijkamp (eds.), *Economy and Ecology: Towards Sustainable Development*, Dordrecht: Kluwer Academic Publishers, pp.203–20.

Newbery, M.G. and J.E. Stiglitz, 1981, *The Theory of Commodity Price Stabilisation – A Study in the Economics of Risk*, Oxford: Clarendon.

Opschoor, J., 1990, 'Environmental Policy Instruments – Experiences with Economic Incentives', in B. Aniansson and U. Svedin (eds.), *Towards an Ecologically Sustainable Economy*, Report from a policy seminar, Stockholm.

Opschoor, J. and J. Vos, 1989, *Economic Instruments for Environmental Protection*, Paris: OECD.

Pearce, D., Barbier, E. and A. Markandya, 1990, *Sustainable Development – Economics and environment in the Third World*, London: Earthscan.

Pezzey, J., 1988, 'Market Mechanisms of Pollution Control: "Polluter Pays", Economic and Practical Aspects', in R.K. Turner (ed.), *Sustainable Environmental Management: Principles and Practice*, Boulder, CO: Westview Press.

Pigou, A., 1920, *The Economics of Welfare*, London: Macmillan, 1950.

Poore, D., 1989, *No Timber Without Trees: Sustainability in the Tropical Forest*, London: Earthscan.

Prestre, Ph. Le, 1989, *The World Bank and the Environmental Challenge*, London: Associated University Press.

Redclift, M., 1989, 'The Environmental Consequences of Latin America's Agricultural Development: Some Thoughts on the Brundtland Commission Report', *World Development*, 17 (3), 365–77.

Repetto, R., Wells, M. Beer, C. and F. Rossini, 1987, 'Natural Resource Accounting for Indonesia', World Resources Institute, Washington.

Siebert, H., 1987, *Economics of the Environment*, second and revised edition, Berlin: Springer.

Stein, R. and G. Grenville-Wood, 1985, 'The Settlement of Environmental Disputes: A Forward Look', Report to the WCED, New York.

Swaminathan, M. *et al.*, 1987, *Food 2000: Global Policies for Sustainable Agriculture, Report to the World Commission on Environment and Development*, London: Zed Press.

Turner, R.K. (ed.), 1988, *Sustainable Environmental Management: Principles and Practice*, Boulder, CO: Westview Press.

UNCTAD, 1990a, 'Review of the Commodity Situation and Outlook 1990', Document TD/B/C.1/309, Geneva.

UNCTAD, 1990b, *Handbook of International Trade and Development Statistics 1989*, New York: United Nations.

UNCTAD, 1990c, '*Sustainable Development and UNCTAD Activities*', Document TD/B/1267, Geneva.

UNCTAD, 1989, 'Identification of Sectors Offering Opportunities for Diversification and Increased Participation of Developing Countries in Processing, Marketing and Distribution', Document TD/B/C.1/AC/7, Geneva.

UNCTAD, 1983, 'International Tropical Timber Agreement 1983', Document TD/TIMBER/11, UNCTAD, Geneva.

UNCTC, 1985, 'Environmental Aspects of the Activities of Transnational Corporations: A Survey', United Nations Center on Transnational Corporations, New York.

Walter, I. and J. Loudon, 1986, 'Environmental Costs and the Patterns of North–South Trade', Paper prepared for the World Commission on Environment and Development, UN, New York.

Wicke, L. and J. Hucke, 1989, *Der Oekologische Marshallplan*, Frankfurt am Main: Ullstein Verlag.

World Bank, 1989, *Sub-Saharan Africa: From Crisis to Sustainable Growth: A Long-Term Perspective Study*, Washington: IBRD.

World Commission on Environment and Development (WCED), 1987, *Our Common Future*, Oxford: University Press.

WRI and IIED, 1986, *World Resources 1986: An Assessment of the Resource Base that Supports the Global Economy*, New York: Basic Books for World Resources Institute and International Institute for Environment and Development.

Climate, Environment and Development

Jan van Ettinger, T. Hans Jansen and Catrinus J. Jepma*

I. INTRODUCTION

This article was prepared as a paper for the large-scale Ministerial Conference on Atmospheric Pollution and Climate Change, organised by UNEP and WMO, together with The Netherlands' government in November 1989. Together with four other papers it supplied background information to the conference, which finally produced the 'Noordwijk Declaration on Climate Change'. Clearly the Noordwijk Conference was just one step in the ongoing process of discussion and political decision-making on the topic of climatic change. Some comparable meetings have followed since. Due to both the interdisciplinary and international aspects of the topic, decision-making is extremely complex and time consuming. If one aspect has become clear, however, it is that one must seek to reach agreement about internationally accepted standards about greenhouse gas emissions, and that the developing countries will play an increasingly important role in finding solutions to the problem.

So, this article deals with global 'climate' related problems of the 'environment', with special attention to the effects on 'development'. In doing so, no attempt will be made to contribute to a further understanding

*Jan van Ettinger and T. Hans Jansen are private consultants; Catrinus J. Jepma is Professor of Economics (University of Groningen and Open University, The Netherlands). Contact address: Jepma, Department of Economics, University of Groningen, PO Box 800, 9700 AV Groningen, The Netherlands. Revised version of a paper presented to the 6th EADI General Conference in Oslo, June 1990. An earlier version constituted a Background Document for the Noordwijk Ministerial Conference on Atmospheric Pollution and Climatic Change organised by the Minister of Housing, Physical Planning and Environment of The Netherlands in co-operation with UNEP and WMO, 6–7 November 1989. The authors wish to thank the many persons who have assisted them by providing relevant literature or giving constructive criticism and valuable suggestions. Special mention should be made here, in alphabetical order, of Lars Björkbom, Antony J. Dolman (for editorial help), Professor Carl-Göran Hedén, M.S. Kismadi and Dr Bo Wiman (for detailed reviewing). Although this article – as well as its predecessor of which it constitutes an elaboration – could never have been written without their invaluable assistance, its shortcomings remain the sole responsibility of the authors.

of the functioning of the global climate system as such, nor of the measures required to address the increasingly urgent problem of development as a whole. Measures to be proposed, however, will aim at protecting the global climate and, thus, at safeguarding an essential condition for sustainable development.

One of the most important global climate problems is the 'greenhouse effect' – rising global surface temperatures and sea levels, and more frequent droughts, hurricanes and floods – due to rapidly increasing atmospheric concentrations of carbon dioxide (CO_2) and of other greenhouse gases. The world's climatologists have reached near consensus that some global warming will be inevitable, even if the emissions of greenhouse gases would be so reduced that their atmospheric concentrations would eventually be stabilised at the current (1988) levels.

Given the long lead times for effective measures, the initiation of action cannot wait until remaining uncertainties as to time, place and extent of the greenhouse effect have been resolved. In view of these uncertainties, however, any course of action should not only be long term and global but also highly flexible in character. This article will discuss measures to mitigate the – as yet insufficiently predictable – impacts of climate change as well as measures to reduce net emissions of greenhouse gases. It will illustrate that without a well-designed internationally coordinated plan of action involving the developing countries, one cannot even hope to solve the issue of global climatic change. A massive North–South transfer as a major component of such a plan is imperative.

In this perspective, the interactions between *Climate Change and Development* will be reviewed in section II. Special attention will be given to potential adverse effects of ocean warming and sea level rise and of increasing climate variability for development, in particular for agricultural production in the developing countries.

Although uncertainties as to the distribution of the effects of climate change remain, section III will discuss *Measures to Mitigate Impacts*. Attention will be given to agriculture, forestry and fishery, to improving infrastructure, and to accelerating socio-economic development. Some observations will be made on the costs of adaptation measures. Section IV will treat *Measures to Reduce Emission Levels*. Given the remaining uncertainties and costs involved, primary attention will be given to measures in areas where other, environmental and/or economic, benefits can be obtained: energy use, deforestation and phasing out CFCs. Some conclusions will be drawn on the cost-effectiveness of the various measures in these areas.

Section V will consider *Climate Change: A 'Common Concern of Mankind'*. It will develop a minimum and maximum CO_2 reduction scenario and estimate the costs of the latter. Finally, some observations will be made on a Climate Fund, which would enable the developing countries, without hampering their economic growth, to play to the full their role in the necessary global co-operation.

Definitions

- *Global climate system.* The global climate results from interactions between insolation, physical and chemical processes in the atmosphere-ocean-ice system, and the world's biota. It manifests itself regionally through (a) mean values of temperature, moisture, insolation, wind speeds and directions; (b) seasonal changes in these mean values; and (c) variability in these parameters, mostly characterised by their extremes.
- *Greenhouse effect and gases.* There is near scientific consensus that global warming will take place due to the combined effect of increasing atmospheric concentrations of the main 'greenhouse gases'. These gases are: carbon dioxide (CO_2), methane (CH_4), ozone (O_3), nitrous oxide (N_2O), and chlorofluorocarbons (CFCs) and others. They contribute roughly 50 per cent, 16 per cent, eight per cent, six per cent and 20 per cent respectively to the global warming likely to occur between 1980 and 2030.
- *Energy sources and conservation.* Energy sources can be divided into renewables and non-renewables. Renewable energy sources are those which are virtually inexhaustible, whereas the total available amount of non-renewable energy sources will decrease if energy is used. Conservation includes all measures aimed at reducing the demand for all sources of energy, especially that for non-renewables.
- *Sustainable development.* The 'Brundtland report' (1987) defines it as 'development that meets the needs of the present without compromising the ability of future generations to meet their own needs. It contains within it two key concepts:
    * the concept of 'needs', in particular the essential needs of the world's poor, to which overriding priority should be given; and
    * the idea of limitations imposed by the state of technology and social organisation on the environment's ability to meet present and future needs.'
- *Developing Countries (DCs) and Industrialised Countries (ICs).* The term DCs refers to the UN grouping of developing countries, incl. the socialist countries of Asia; ICs encompasses the UN categories of developed market economies and the socialist countries of Eastern Europe and the USSR.

Units: A Note

Each form of energy has been converted in its conventional fuel equivalent. Energy data of supporting sources are put in ExaJoule (EJ) or GigaJoule (GJ); for end-uses the more popular unit Watt (Watt year per year) has been used. Greenhouse gas emissions are expressed in GigaTon of Carbon (GTC) equivalent and investment costs in US dollars per Ton Carbon equivalent saved ($/TC). Finally, where Ton Carbon Dioxide (TCD) is used as a unit: 1 TCD = 3.66 TC.

1 EJ	$= 10^{18}$ Joule	1 GTC	$= 10^9$ Ton Carbon
1 GJ	$= 10^9$ Joule	1 EJ biomass	~ 0.031 GTC $\times$ 2
1 W	= 0.0315 GJ per year	1 EJ coal	~ 0.027 GTC
1 billion	$= 10^3$ million	1 EJ oil	~ 0.020 GTC
1 hectare	= 10,000 m^2 = 2.471 acres	1 EJ natural gas	~ 0.014 GTC

II. CLIMATE CHANGE AND DEVELOPMENT

Climate Change

Over the past ten million years, clouds, water vapour, and pre-industrial concentrations of CO_2 together warmed the earth's surface by some 33 °C, from an estimated average temperature of −18 °C to around +15 °C. Without this background greenhouse effect, the earth would be a cold and lifeless planet.

In former times mankind faced many climate changes and developed many adjustment strategies. Man has dared to go to the limits of all climates. The way of coping with major climate change, if it did not lead to the extinction of complete civilisations, was massive migration. Today this option is no longer a feasible one. There is a lack of the space required for it and growing urban populations are firmly tied to past investments of money and imagination.

What has only relatively recently become known with respect to climate change, however, is the following:

– Man-made emissions of CO_2, especially from burning fossil fuels and biomass, and of other trace gases do increase their atmospheric concentrations, thus affecting the global greenhouse.
– Global warming also results from emissions of greenhouse gases during the 'fuel cycle' (mining, transport, etc.) and from a decrease in the amount of CO_2 stored in the biosphere due to, significantly increasing, devegetation.

- Since 1800 the earth has experienced a 0.5–0.7 °C warming. Computer simulations, supported by analyses of the age and CO_2-content of Antartic ice masses, suggest a doubling of the CO_2 concentration will lead to a warming of 1.5–4.5 °C.
- Studies indicate large time-lags between emissions, increases in atmospheric concentrations and global warming. If emissions were stabilised at the present levels, the greenhouse effect would still intensify for more than a century.
- After stopping CO_2 emissions, it would take more than 50 years for the oceans (when warmer, their absorptive capacity even decreases) to absorb enough CO_2 to bring its atmospheric concentration halfway down to its pre-industrial level.

This leads to the conclusion that drastic cuts in emissions of greenhouse gases are required. A reduction of at least 50 per cent is needed to eventually stabilise their atmospheric concentrations at present levels. Measures to reduce emissions of greenhouse gases should be complemented by those that stop devegetation and restore the earth's absorptive capacity.

Climate Change and Development

Since the discovery in 1985 of the 'hole' in the ozone layer over Antarctica, the awareness of the potential for rapid and surprising shifts in the climate system has strongly increased. The appearance of the 'Brundtland Report' in 1987 highlighted the until then largely neglected socio-economic implications of climate change. This new focus emphasised the need for a fundamentally new perception of the risks and uncertainties involved. Thus, the wait-and-see policy attitude characteristic of the 1970s has changed to one of finding policy strategies and measures capable of buying the time needed to understand and manage the mutual interactions between climate and development. With respect to these interactions the following three issues can be discerned:

(a) To what extent does climate change, as a result of the greenhouse effect, already take place in the DCs and, if so, in which ways does it manifest itself?

(b) If climate change does take place in the DCs, what will its impact be on agriculture, forestry, water management, fisheries, energy use, urbanisation, and well-being? In short, what are its direct socio-economic consequences?

(c) If there are direct consequences, what do they mean for such economic variables as labour mobility, patterns of production, international trade, external indebtedness, in short, for the overall process of development?

The literature consulted shows that our present insight into (a) is limited, though less so than in (b), and certainly less than in (c). This insight is crucial for identifying the investments required and the cost likely to be incurred in combating the effects of climate change and preventing its further escalation. Hence, much additional research on the above issues is needed.

The generally unstable socio-economic situation in the DCs, their scarcity of alternative opportunities for production, and the fact that often seventy per cent of their household energy use is for cooking on biomass with a low efficiency, makes climate change a serious development problem. This is further aggravated because the impact of climate change on a resource system (such as energy and water) will obviously be largest where the resource is already scarce or poorly managed, as is the case in many DCs.

The Greenhouse Effect and DCs

Special attention for the problems posed to the DCs does not mean to say that those posed to the ICs could be ignored. On the contrary, the temperature rises at higher latitudes may even be two or three times as large as in the tropics.

Ocean warming and sea level rise: The oceans reduce the speed of global warming, by their large mass and thermal inertia, but will gradually become warmer themselves. The resulting thermal expansion alone would lead to a substantial sea level rise. It is expected, however, that global warming will also lead to melting of the ice caps, as well as to changed patterns of ocean circulation in the upper layers and of up- and down-welling. Even if the precise impacts of these phenomena in DCs remain unclear, it is not difficult to imagine what they may mean for risks of flooding, for fishery resources, for salt water intrusion into fresh-water aquifers, and for wetlands and other productive ecosystems.

A rise in sea level will seriously affect developing regions barely above sea level. This specifically holds for large deltas, like in Bangladesh, Egypt and parts of China, and low island groups, such as the Maldives. Their existence is threatened since they may be flooded, unless they are protected by dikes and other infrastructure. Constructing such protection will be costly and sometimes technically impossible. The costs of a one metre rise in the height of dikes in the Netherlands are estimated at $5 billion; the World Bank puts the costs of a substantial sea level rise protection plan for Bangladesh at $6 billion.

According to the Worldwatch Institute, sea level rise could become the primary cause of 'environmental refugees' by the middle of the next century. Populations exposed to natural hazards are the most vulnerable.

In 2050, habitable land might well be lost for 15 per cent in Bangladesh and Egypt. The part of their populations displaced could amount to 13 per cent.

Sea level rise will also lead to changes in 'baselines' and thus sea borders, for example, of Exclusive Economic Zones. Even if only one uninhabited island were to be flooded, this could still have serious economic consequences because of a reduction of the ocean resources of the nation-state in question.

Climate variability: Another, but much less predictable, impact of the greenhouse effect is a change in climate variability. Even though one cannot yet conclude that such climate change is already taking place (because changes have so far remained within natural fluctuation margins), simulation models strongly point in this direction. Moreover, circumstantial evidence is, for instance, provided by the 1987 monsoon failure in India, and the progressive Sahel desertification.

The impact on DCs can be considerable, given the generally vulnerable state of their infrastructure. More variability in rainfall, more frequent hurricanes, droughts, etc. can have catastrophic implications. If the amount and intensity of precipitation change, this may affect soil moisture conditions and enhance soil erosion and desertification processes, thus aggravating existing problems.

Water resources are also highly sensitive to climate variations. Wet spells, droughts, floods and more frequent hurricanes can affect the availability of water for agriculture, drinking and power generation, as well as river navigation, fisheries, and tourism. The key problem in projecting climate change in DCs is that results of climate models, though fairly unanimous about the threat of enlarged climate variability, differ significantly in regional detail.

Insight into impacts of climate change on average yields has grown recently. Simulation models, for instance, have shown for a number of crops in ICs that changes in the level of productivity are related to changes in mean temperature and precipitation. These models could be applied to DC agriculture, but this has not yet been done systematically. Much less is known about the impact of climate variability. However, available information suggests that its impact on agricultural production could be in the order of some tens of per cents.

The impact of climate change on forests is also poorly understood, although forest simulation models have been used to assess the impact of temperature change on wood or biomass. The problem is again that changes in regional moisture patterns – which are still the least known – rather than in mean temperatures are usually the determining factor.

Agricultural production: Discussion of consequences for agriculture is more informed for cool-temperate and cold areas, where temperature rather than rainfall is the major climatic determinant, than for semi-arid regions, where moisture is the primary climatic constraint. The majority of DCs belong to the latter category. DCs with precarious food supplies and a degradation of land resources appear to be especially vulnerable to climate change. Moreover, they usually lack the resources to combat adverse effects or to profit from beneficial effects of climate change.

It is probable that low-latitude, semi-arid developing regions will experience changes in rainfall. This calls for a reappraisal of the recent emphasis on high-yielding cultivars and crop production, which has discouraged diversified, flexible and low-risk production systems prevalent in traditional agriculture. These high-yielding systems have evolved to a state where they can support vast populations, but are tolerant of only small changes in temperature and water and can probably not be adapted very quickly to significant climate changes.

III. MEASURES TO MITIGATE IMPACTS

Introduction

Although uncertainties remain as to the distribution in space and time of mean values and frequency and intensity of extreme events, climate change may be the fastest ever faced by mankind. Anticipatory action is, therefore, imperative. The measures to be taken fall under the following two categories:

- *adaptation* to climate change (or *effect-oriented* measures): to better protect against or to lower vulnerability to the adverse effects during production, distribution and consumption and to better use beneficial effects, if any; and
- *limitation* of climate change (or *source-oriented* measures): to reduce the increase of atmospheric concentrations of CO_2 and other greenhouse gases, by the prevention or absorption (including capture and disposal) of their emissions.

These two categories are interlinked. The more one succeeds in limiting climate change, the easier it will be to adapt to it and vice versa. Adaptation to climate will be discussed before limitation of climate change. This is not done to suggest an order of priority, quite the contrary. *Climate change may remain manageable only if enough source-oriented measures* are soon taken to buy time.

Three types of 'adaptation' measures will be distinguished: (i) mitigation of impacts on agriculture, forestry and fisheries; (ii) improving infrastructure; (iii) accelerating socio-economic development.

Mitigation of Impacts on Agriculture, Forestry and Fisheries

Agriculture: How can agriculture (including animal husbandry) best adapt to climate change? Preparing for climate change should start with better adjustment to the usual climate and its variability. In Mali, for example, a pilot project demonstrated that farmers using advice on how to profit from information on the effects of weather and climate increased production in drought years by 25–30 per cent. But, among DCs, so far only South East Asia has a regional climate data base.

Various types of technical responses are available: change in crop variety; change in irrigation, fertiliser and drainage; change in crop management; and change in farming strategies. Salt-tolerant crops (halophytes) deserve special mention. Some of them can be very successfully grown along the shore-line of coastal deserts when irrigated with ocean water. When this comes from shrimp farms, a waste water problem is solved and a crop is fertilised all in one.

Given our still limited understanding of climate change, however, the focus should be on *extending the range of policy options* rather than on refining technical responses. In this respect, the following policy options deserve to be considered: changes in land-use allocation; in farm support, and food security policies; reduction of post-harvest losses; developing potential of tropical (plant) species; and conversion to 'controlled environment agriculture'.

Changes in land-use allocation would include changes to optimise (different crops respond differently to climate change) and to stabilise production (reducing the risks of heavy losses). National farm support policies have to be adapted specifically to encourage different types of farm management and levels of input to match climate induced changes in agricultural potential. National food security policies must be reviewed against possible climate change, especially in DCs with precarious food supplies.

Post-harvest losses – due to deficient systems of storage and transport, during which food is vulnerable to rodents and to perishing – amount in many DCs to 50 per cent or more. Most of the world's plant food comes from only 20 species, so the potential of the vast majority of plant species has still to be developed. As to mammals, for example, 'natural ranching' (Kenya) appears to offer great promise. Another fundamental way to mitigate impacts could be to make agriculture 'independent' from the climate via 'controlled environment agriculture'.

Forestry: As far as forestry is concerned, it should be recognised that the growing cycles of trees are some 10–100 times longer than those of food crops. Many of the measures applicable to agriculture cannot or can hardly be used for forestry. Because of their CO_2 absorption capacity – and other vital functions like soil protection, rainwater catchment, and safeguarding of genetic diversity – existing forests should be protected against deforestatation (currently 11 million hectares per year) and climate change by local measures. These should, as far as possible, respect the legitimate rights of local people.

Fisheries: Climate effects on marine fisheries are hard to quantify, because of large natural fluctuations, human intervention, and generally poor data on fish populations. Climate change affects ocean circulation in the upper layers, upwelling and ice extent, all of which affect marine biological production and hence marine fisheries. Efforts to adapt marine fisheries to climate change should be complemented by intensified efforts to develop *aquaculture*; its potential for satisfying the world's protein needs is still largely unutilised.

Integrating aquaculture with 'controlled environment agriculture' has a great potential. In recent years, dramatic advances in marine biotechnology have been made. The almost sterile, nutrient-rich bottom water from OTEC-systems promises much as culture medium for kelp, abalone, oysters and a range of fish species.

Improving Infrastructure

To cope with the impacts of climate on development, infrastructure should be adapted in particular to changed precipitation – in terms of mean value and variability – as well as to higher sea levels. This especially concerns irrigation/water storage systems, including (small) dams, drainage/sewer systems, dikes and locks, as well as urban building and construction.

Water resource development and management forms one of the most important life-sustaining activities. The rate of expansion of irrigation has varied over time. It peaked in the early 1970s and is now decreasing. Future irrigation investments in DCs should be specifically targeted at countries with persistent food deficits. Water is also needed for drinking and cooking, and for power production. Climate change may have large cumulative effects on water storage systems, particularly if their present capacity is approaching design limits.

Sea level rise, especially if attended with floods or hurricanes, may seriously affect deltas, wetlands, estuaries and low islands. Measures should be taken to prevent a loss of land and an increase in salinity. If sea borders of island states are affected, for example, of Exclusive Economic Zones, legal measures (ongoing recognition) rather than technical ones (endiking) may have to be taken. The 'heat island' produced by large cities at night is already a well-known phenomenon. With increasing mean and extreme temperatures, a reorganisation of cities could be needed to prevent excessive heat accumulation and to facilitate cooling. Cost-effective means of alleviating urban climate extremes should be part of a strategy to reduce energy demands. Options that could be considered include reducing the need for air conditioning by planting trees, switching to lighter coloured surfaces and making use of passive solar heating concepts.

Settlement planning will need to anticipate the long-term spatial effects of climate change (in mean values and extremes). This is of particular importance to countries with vulnerable coast-lines or different climate types (such as Brazil, India and China). Given the long lifetime of buildings and urban infrastructure, it will be a hard challenge to successfully introduce into physical planning the increasingly needed notions of discontinuity and surprise.

Accelerating Socio-economic Development

Accelerating socio-economic development in the DCs will prove to be of vital importance to reduce their vulnerability to climate change, because:

- eradication of mass poverty, especially in the rural areas, is imperative to redress the present imbalance between resources and population. This imbalance enhances processes of dry land degradation and deforestation.
- agriculture (1986: in DCs 19 per cent and in ICs three per cent of GNP) is the most climate sensitive economic sector. To decrease overall vulnerability to climate change, development of the industry and services sectors should be accelerated.
- with the level of socio-economic development, the availability of financial and human resources will increase. These resources can, in part, be allocated to better adapting to climate change as well as to limiting climate change.
- higher levels of education and well-being have been shown to be a *conditio sine qua non* for effective population planning policies. The latter are crucial for redressing on the long-run present imbalances between population and resources.
- an increase in the availability of modern telecommunications enhances mass information capabilities. Their importance is illustrated by the action of UNDRO, which reduced the effects of hurricane Gilbert (1988) in the Caribbean.

Costs of Adaptation Measures

The way to adapt to climate change may be 'controlled environment agriculture'. Cheap materials, simple construction techniques, and micro-biological systems would be combined to make agriculture + aquaculture 'independent' from climate change. Massive introduction of such integrated systems in DCs, at $250 per capita as a 'ballpark' estimate, would require an investment of $1,000 billion, or $25 billion per year over a 40-year period. This long-term option, however, needs much further research: large-scale 'engineering the unknown (that is, Nature) out of the system' may prove to be ecologically and economically vulnerable.

Measures to better protect against or lower vulnerability to climate change may be costly and can only effectively be taken after the distribution of its effects has become predictable. Accelerating socio-economic development of DCs will, in any case, prove to be vital to lower their vulnerability. Measures to this end belong to 'development co-operation' rather than to climate change policies. To 'buy time', so as to clear the remaining uncertainties, in actual investments, highest priority should be given to limitation of climate change.

IV. MEASURES TO REDUCE EMISSION LEVELS

To 'buy time', measures should be taken to reduce emission levels of greenhouse gases. However, given the remaining uncertainties at to climate change, these measures should primarily be taken in areas where other, environmental and/or economic, benefits can be obtained. Three such areas are the following:

– *energy use*, which is vital for development: its reduction will contribute to combating acid rain and smog, will save on energy expenditures and imports;
– *deforestation*, which is often needed to survive: its halting will help combat desertification and erosion processes, and extinction of genetic species;
– *phasing out of CFCs*: if also done in DCs, this will speed up the reversing of the process of the depletion of the ozone layer.

The main greenhouse gases are: carbon dioxide (CO_2), methane (CH_4), ozone (O_3), nitrous oxide (N_2O), and chlorofluorocarbons (CFCs). Their emissions are caused by the following sectors of activity: energy, deforestation, agriculture, and industry. Table 1 gives estimates of the contribution of each gas and sector to the global warming *likely to occur between 1980 and 2030*.

TABLE 1

GASES/SECTORS OF GOBAL WARMING

sector / gas	carbon dioxide (CO_2)	methane (CH_4)	ozone (O_3)	nitrous oxide (N_2O)	chlorofluorocarbons (CFCs+)	per cent warming sector
energy	35	4^x	6^x	4		49
deforestation	10	4				14
agriculture	3	8		2		13
industry	2		2		20	24
per cent warming gas	50	16	8	6	20	100

+) and others   x) of which 1and 6 per cent points indirect, respectively

Source: World Resources Institute, 1988.

Energy use and *deforestation* together cause 63 per cent of the global warming likely to occur between 1980 and 2030. Including phasing out CFCs brings this to 83 per cent. Thus, by concentrating in the first instance on these three areas, not more than 17 per cent of the emissions are ignored. Moreover, the sources of and limitation measures for these emissions, especially of CH_4 from agriculture, are still insufficiently known.

Measures to reduce net emission levels of greenhouse gases, caused by the use of energy and by deforestation, should be distinguished in two categories:

Measures to prevent emissions:
- energy saving and efficiency;
- combustible fuel switch; and
- use of alternative energy sources.

Measures to absorb emissions:
- reafforestation; and
- CO_2 capture and disposal.

Measures to Prevent Emissions

Energy saving and efficiency: Significant gains can be achieved, both in ICs and DCs, by a strategy focussing on the improvement of end-uses of energy. The scope for energy saving in the ICs already manifested itself: in 1973–84 industrial production increased over 30 per cent, whereas energy use hardly expanded. For example, a study shows that the US could cut, over the next two decades, its energy consumption in half without reducing its living standards. This would save $50 billion [*Keepin et al., 1988*].

There is great potential for increased energy efficiency in DCs, since it is the most cost-effective means of dealing with a rapid growth in energy demand. According to a 1986 study of Brazil, $10 billion investments in electric energy efficiency – in more efficient refrigerators, lighting, etc. – would offset the need for $40 billion investments in power generation [*Goldenberg et al., 1987*]. The energy-saving scope in the three main sectors of use – households, transportation and industry – will be explored for the period up to 2005 and beyond.

Households: ICs use some 25–35 per cent of their energy in households, primarily for heating. From studies it can be concluded that per capita energy consumption in households could be reduced by half, with available techniques, without loss of comfort. An example of potential gains is fluorescent lighting, which is more than four times as efficient as the incandescent bulb and lasts ten times as long. Of the 800 W per capita remaining in 2005 after energy saving (1988: 1,400 W), for lighting, cooking and leisure 300 W would be used and for heating 500 W. The widespread use of advanced solar heating techniques could eventually provide 80 per cent of the energy for heating and cooling.

DCs use 60–80 per cent of their energy in households, the level of which varies considerably between countries and between urban and rural regions. Some 70 per cent of energy in households – 500 W per capita as an average – is derived from fuelwood for cooking with a very low efficiency. Existing technology has the potential to reduce energy use in households to 300 W per capita, the same as required for a western standard of living in terms of lighting, cooking and leisure. Because the transition to commercial energy will take time, a reduction to only 400 W per capita appears achievable by 2005. Thereafter, a further reduction could be achieved through decentralised (solar) energy and continued development of the infrastructure for commercial energy.

Transportation: In 1982 passenger cars – whose use is considered to be representative for the transport sector as a whole – consumed about one sixth of global oil output. Improved fuel economy could have a significant impact on oil use in both ICs and DCs. Strict emission rules on the one hand and higher fuel prices on the other have resulted in the development of a new generation of cars. Cars with a fuel consumption of four litres per 100 km are available, at only a ten per cent higher price, while the average car in the US still consumes as much as $14\frac{1}{2}$ litres per 100 km. Reducing fuel consumption of all American cars by about one-half would already eliminate all US oil imports from OPEC!

Cars are rapidly becoming a major oil user in DCs. In recent years, their number has increased by 7.3 per cent per year, compared to 2.6 per cent in ICs. In many DCs oil for transport consumes the major part of their foreign-exchange earnings. DCs should take the lead in using high economy cars, perhaps even in producing them, to reduce oil imports. Shifting to public transport can only have a large impact where the occupation rate of private cars is low. Increased availability of modern telecommunications could reduce future mobility needs.

Industry: Energy efficiency improvements in industry have been pursued throughout history. Major examples are in steel making, the oil industry and the power sector. Detailed studies of different industrial branches in ICs indicate, that by utilising advanced technology the industry could reduce energy use (relative to value added) to half its present level. The main share of the large industrial energy intensity reductions in IEA countries in 1973–84 – 30 per cent or some three per cent per year – were made 'autonomously' as the capital stock was gradually renewed. The large value of the reduction during this period may have been positively affected by the adjustments which followed the oil crises.

The energy efficiency improvements of total production – two per cent per year during the same, probably exceptional, period – are less than of industry alone. Historically, one finds lower figures for the 'autonomous' annual reduction in overall energy intensity, usually ranging between one and two per cent. These figures are clearly smaller than the projections for overall economic growth up to 2005 and as such do not allow for reduced total energy use. It can be fairly concluded, therefore, that environmental targets can only be achieved if some further obstacles to exploiting efficiency opportunities are removed.

There is evidence that with available technologies – provided that incentives exist for their application – a further increase in efficiency of over 30 per cent can be achieved in industry in the next 15–20 years. Recent projects show, for example, that it costs no more to build an energy-efficient office building than an inefficient one. Some studies indicate that with advanced technologies energy efficiency increases of 60 per cent or more could still be realised. In ICs, with appropriate policy adjustments, a reduction in per capita energy use in 2005 to 4,400 W seems to be within reach; this would mean a total energy use of 194 EJ. In DCs, an increase in the per capita energy use in 2005 to only 1,020 W seems possible; this would mean a total energy use of 167 EJ.

Our end-use analysis of energy shows that economic growth, both in DCs and ICs, could be achieved up to 2005 without increasing global energy use beyond its present level if a shift is made to modern energy saving techniques. This highlights the opportunities for DCs of technological 'leap-frogging', if they select less resource-intensive and environmentally-destructive technologies.

The following factors prevent the above potential from being realised:

- obstacles to correct economic pricing of traditional forms of energy and a lack of policies to ensure correct economic signals;
- in sufficient funds for energy research and development, and slow application of results by government organisations;
- more than 90 per cent of investments go to large energy generating systems, whereas conservation accounted for less than one per cent; and
- a lack of awareness among the general public and private enterprise of the benefits of and technologies available for energy saving and efficiency.

Combustible fuel switch: Per unit of energy, the CO_2 emissions of coal and oil are respectively two and one-and-a-half times as large as that of natural gas. Fuel switch is thus an option which deserves serious attention, especially since world natural gas reserves are surpassing those of oil. The rate of global introduction of natural gas, however, will be limited by exploration and transportation constraints. The environmental advantages of switching to natural gas can be reduced by leakage (measured by the Battelle Institute in the FRG to be below 0.7 per cent of consumption), CH_4 being some fourteen times as harmful as CO_2 in contributing to the greenhouse effect.

Strict technology and rules for handling natural gas are thus needed. Natural gas has further environmental advantages (for example, very low emissions of sulphur dioxide). Besides, infrastructure for its distribution (pipelines) and its combustion (advanced gas turbines) can also be used for gas from biomass or coal-gasification, and, in future, increasingly for hydrogen.

The contribution of biomass, per unit of energy, to the greenhouse effect is at least two times that of coal, if no compensation for the corresponding loss in CO_2 absorption capacity is made. In DCs the switch to kerosine and gas for cooking and from kerosene to fluorescent lamps for lighting should, also for for reasons of efficiency improvement, be carried out as soon as possible.

Combining new technologies for coal-gasification with those for CO_2 capture and disposal (see section on CO_2 capture and disposal below), to replace direct use of coal for power generation, requires further development and may not generally be applied before 2005.

Use of alternative energy sources: The role of nuclear energy is not expected to grow globally. Even if its well-known problems – like the storage of nuclear waste, threats of nuclear terrorism and proliferation of nuclear weapons technology – are accepted, it is a relatively expensive option for displacing carbon. CO_2-emission reduction, per monetary unit invested, by nuclear energy has been calculated, under fairly realistic assumptions, to be less by a factor of 7 than that achieved by energy saving. Although changing these assumptions does have an impact on this factor (it ranges from 2½–10), the nuclear option remains one of the least cost-effective ones. As to (cold) nuclear *fusion*, it still has a long way (2030 or beyond) to go.

The slow rate of implementation of other non-combustion energy systems is partly caused by the large capital investments required and the associated risks involved. This is illustrated by the experience with large hydro-projects in DCs during periods of fluctuating energy prices. The inherently small-scale character of the main part of other non-combustible sources of energy – such as solar heating, photo-voltaics and wind power – is another drawback. A final impediment is the widespread application in DCs of subsidies on some forms of energy which discourage R&D of and investments in alternative sources.

Measures to Absorb Emissions

Reafforestation: Deforestation occurs at an annual rate of 11 million hectares against one million only for reafforestation. Due to deforestation 1–3 GT carbon is released annually (compared to six GT from 1988 global fossil fuels use) and thousands of genetic species are extinguished. Halting deforestation and increasing reafforestation would largely contribute to balancing the atmospheric CO_2 concentration.

A massive reafforestation plan, to compensate for ongoing deforestation and to absorb an average of three GTC/year, of 750 million hectares in 40 years would cost (based on World Bank data) some $6 billion per year. In terms of investments, reafforestation is the most effective ($2/TC) measure to reduce CO_2 emissions.

There are, however, some caveats. First, these forests should not be turned into future (fuel)wood reserves. Second, it is assumed that all arising social, legal, and institutional land use problems can be overcome. Third, reafforestation has only a longer term (after some 20 years) net effect and may show dis-economies of scale. Given these caveats, for the immediate future reafforestation should be considered as an important but not as a major policy option.

CO_2 capture and disposal: CO_2 capture and disposal techniques are as yet insufficiently developed and their general use in power plants cannot

be expected before 2005. Present indications are that, when advanced technology is installed, new power plants could capture and dispose of their CO_2 emissions at $60–130/TC. This would prevent emission until their eventual, inadvertent or wilful, release. If made mandatory for coal-fired plants, resulting electricity price increases would positively effect energy conservation. The further development of clean coal technologies (CO_2 capture and disposal combined with coal gasification) is of great intermediate potential, especially for coal rich countries such as China.

Phasing Out Chlorofluorocarbons (CFCs)

CFCs contribute some 20 per cent to global warming. Their phasing out globally ranks high on the international agenda, given the increasing concerns over the ozone layer. It could be carried out relatively 'easily', as compared to, say, the restructuring of global energy policy, and is considered to be very cost-effective, if at least CFCs are not replaced by HFCs (greenhouse gases).

Conclusions

- Dealing with CFCs and reafforestation appears, in terms of investments, to be the most cost-effective policy for the short and long term respectively.
- Given uncertainties as to cost structure and differences in impact of other policy options, a mix ('portfolio') of policies should be carefully selected.
- In preventing emissions, energy saving deserves first priority given its CO_2-reduction potential and since it is (largely) a self-paying proposition.
- Fuel switch to natural gas provides a means to buy time in the medium term, alternative energy sources constitute the long-term sustainable option.
- R&D efforts should be increased with respect to the most viable measures to reduce emission levels in the medium and longer term.

V. CLIMATE CHANGE: A 'COMMON CONCERN OF MANKIND'

There are two extreme policy options available for dealing with the greenhouse problem, namely:

- to reduce emission levels of greenhouse gases via 'source-oriented' measures (reduction scenario); or
- to mitigate impacts of future climate change via 'effect-oriented' measures (adaptation scenario).

To effectively deal with the problem, elements of both options must be applied simultaneously. Both options will confront the world with major economic costs. In a reduction scenario, the main costs will be in energy saving and adjustment measures. In an adaptation scenario climate change itself will determine the costs. There is a clear trade-off between the costs of both scenarios.

The following estimates of the costs associated with the various measures of both options are necessarily rather rough and only serve to draw some initial conclusions on the cost-effectiveness of the various measures. Finally, the information will be translated into suggestions with respect to a Climate Fund.

Costs of an Adaptation Scenario

In an adaptation scenario the emphasis is placed on adapting to climate change and compensating for the damage it causes. Various reasoned guesses have been made of the damage that may occur, but they should be considered 'ballpark' estimates. One estimate assumes that only agriculture will suffer a loss: some ten per cent of its output. This would mean damages in DCs in the order of $50 billion per year. Another study estimates the damage at three per cent of global production or at some $400 billion per year for the world as a whole (excluding CMEA countries), of which $75 billion per year in the DCs (1988 prices).

Damages in DCs will probably be relatively larger than in ICs, because the agricultural sector (in 1986: in DCs 19 per cent of GNP, in ICs three per cent) is more vulnerable to climate change. Yields in DCs can be especially sensitive to changes in precipitation (a study on Kenyan maize production indicated a 15 per cent crop loss when rainfall was ten per cent less than average). If the above three per cent production damages break down into ten per cent in agriculture and two-and-a-half per cent in other sectors, the damages in DCs would amount to some $100 billion per year.

A fundamental way to adapt to climate change might be the widespread application of 'controlled environment agriculture' integrated with aquaculture, thus creating 'greenhouses in the greenhouse'. However, this long-term option needs further research: large-scale approaches to 'engineering the unknown (Nature) out of the system' may prove to be ecologically and economically vulnerable. Dealing with the damages in DCs would require large funds, ranging from $50 to $100 billion per year. Moreover, since this would not halt climate change, its disruptions would increase suffering in DCs, especially in their rural areas.

CO_2 Reduction Scenarios

To eventually stabilise the atmospheric CO_2 concentration at the present high level, a reduction of 1988 emissions with at least 50 per cent will be needed. Such reduction can only be obtained through global co-operation and at considerable costs. Because of these costs, the remaining uncertainties as to climate change are used to argue for continuing studies rather than starting action. Given this lack of political will on the one hand and the need to 'buy time' on the other, two scenarios will be developed, namely: (i) a politically feasible or minimum scenario, in which ICs bring their CO_2 emissions in 2000 back to the 1988 level; and (ii) an environmentally desirable or maximum scenario, in which global CO_2 emissions in 2005 are reduced by 20 per cent compared to 1988. The first reflects the view of many ICs expressed in the Noordwijk Declaration on Climate Change (1989), the second was recommended by the World Conference on the Changing Climate in Toronto (1988). Both scenarios must not be mistaken for projections, they merely show the outcome of certain sets of assumptions.

A politically feasible or minimum scenario:

- ICs bring, as a first step, CO_2 emissions by 2000 back to the 1988 level; they increase natural gas supply to 76 EJ (Committee J: 'rapid scenario'); and non-combustibles supply by two per cent per year during the period 1988–2000.
- DCs extrapolate their 1972–87 energy growth rate (4.8 per cent per year); they increase non-combustibles by two-and-a half per cent per year; and they make no combustible fuel switches during the period 1988–2000.

According to this scenario, the ICs would only increase their total energy use by 0.7 per cent per year, compared to 1.7 per cent per year during the period 1972–87. This is largely explained by their increase per capita energy use, which would amount to only 0.5 per cent in total over 1988–2000.

By 2000, the DCs would have increased their CO_2 emissions by 79 per cent over the 1988 level. With 52 per cent of the total, against 38 per cent in 1988, they would have taken over the role of the ICs as major source of CO_2 emissions. However, the per capita energy use in ICs would still be six times higher than in DCs.

Global CO_2 emissions would still grow to 130 per cent of the 1988 level. Since they should eventually be reduced to at most 50 per cent, this minimum scenario is unacceptable. Therefore, a maximum scenario will be developed according to considerations of environmental desirability rather than political feasibility.

An environmentally desirable or maximum scenario: Global targets for reducing CO_2 emissions and needs of the developing countries (DCs) for increasing fossil fuel use together determine the reduction targets for the industrialised countries (ICs). A scenario has been designed in which the global CO_2 emissions are reduced, compared to 1988, by 20 per cent in 2005.

The main assumptions underlying the scenario are the following:

- global supply of non-combustibles (hydro, nuclear and renewables) increases by three per cent per year in the period 1988–2005;
- the ICs reduce their total energy use, through energy saving and efficiency, by two per cent per year in 1988–2005;
- the DCs increase their total energy use by four per cent per year in 1988–2005, compared to 4.8 per cent in 1972–87.

Given these assumptions, global annual energy use would grow in 1988–2005 from 379 to 395 EJ per year, or in total with four per cent only. If in this period economic growth in the ICs amounts to two-and-a-half per cent per year without energy saving and if the DCs would continue to increase energy use by 4.8 per cent per year, then global energy use would increase from 379 to 648 EJ per year. Thus, in total an energy saving by 2005 is envisaged of 648−395 = 253 EJ per year.

Our end-use analysis, carried out in the section on Energy saving and efficiency, has shown that energy saving and efficiency measures have the potential to reduce annual energy use by the ICs to 194 EJ in 2005 or two per cent below the 197 EJ in the above scenario. Annual energy use by the DCs needs to increase to 167 EJ or 16 per cent below the above 198 EJ. These two points are kept 'in reserve' when concluding that the maximum scenario is not only environmentally desirable but also technically feasible.

Costs of a Reduction Scenario

A reduction scenario can focus on prevention (energy saving; combustible fuel switch; and alternative sources) or absorption (reafforestation; and capture and disposal) of CO_2 emissions. The costs involved in both options are explored below. It should be kept in mind however, that the average costs used can differ substantially from the marginal costs due to (dis)economies of scale.

Energy saving and efficiency: Of the above target for global energy saving of 253 EJ per year in 2005, some 90 EJ would be 'autonomous' or come about without making policy adjustments. Therefore, additional savings up to 163 EJ per year in 2005 should lead to a reduction of 51 per cent (of 1988 CO_2 emissions), or 4.0 GTC. With data of the World Resources Institute, the annual investments needed to achieve these additional savings have been estimated at some $120 billion globally, of which $100 billion for ICs and $20 billion for DCs.

Combustible Fuel switch: Another reduction of CO_2 emissions should be realised by switching from coal and oil to gas. A 13 per cent reduction, or 1.0 GTC, could be achieved if the annual production of natural gas were to increase from 64 EJ in 1988 to 112 EJ in 2005. The corresponding gas supply growth rate of 3.3 per cent per year would require large investments in gas infrastructure. The investment costs of exploration and extraction, and of the extension of the existing network into a global gas distribution system (data from the Dutch Gas Union; average transport distance 2,500 kilometres) would be in the order of $70 billion per year.

Alternative sources: Producing 39 EJ per year from additional alternative sources (hydro, wind, and solar) by 2005 should contribute some 12 per cent, or 0.9 GTC, to reaching the Toronto target. It is estimated that this would require investments of some $110 billion per year. This option is still relatively costly, but economies of scale and new technologies may gradually lower costs. The 'energy/profit ratio' of photovoltaics has, for example, increased from one in 1972 to ten for present complete single-crystal systems; new amorphous cells offer even more promise. In the long run, only alternatives can provide a sustainable energy base.

If it is assumed that no additional investments are involved in 'autonomous' energy savings, the annual investments in energy use reduction would be in the order of $300 billion of which $90 billion in DCs. A limited energy price increase (30 per cent of present global energy costs) would suffice to achieve the Toronto target, provided the revenues are used only to cover the costs of effective energy policy options.

Phasing Out Chlorofluorocarbons (CFCs)

Finally, CFCs, which contribute some 20 per cent to global warming, should be mentioned. Estimates suggest the total annual costs of phasing them out would be in the order of $23 billion, of which $20 billion for ICs and $3 billion for DCs. Such a policy could be carried out relatively 'easily', as compared to say the restructuring of global energy policy. Moreover, its contribution to solving the greenhouse problem is very cost-effective ($10/TC).

CONCLUSION

Dealing with CFCs and reafforestation appear to be the most cost-effective policies for the short and long term respectively. Given uncertainties as to the cost structure of other options and differences in their impact, a mix of policies should be selected. Energy saving deserves much attention given its potential. Fuel switch provides a means to buy time in the medium term, alternative sources constitute the long-term sustainable option.

Annual investments needed to achieve the maximum scenario would amount to some $330 billion, of which $230 billion in the ICs (less than two per cent of their GNP) and $100 billion in DCs (as much as four per cent of their GNP). With such an amount, 83 per cent of global warming (see Table 1) would be addressed.

Given their already towering problems, the vast majority of the DCs could not contribute to combating global warming without hampering their own development. They can only share the burden of global warming if the ICs give them access to additional, public or private, capital and to climate related (high) technology.

The access to additional capital should be on 'concessional terms'. The access to the appropriate (high) technology should, as much as possible, have the form of co-development schemes. Such schemes would not only help to ensure efficient co-operation but also equitable benefit-sharing between ICs and DCs.

The access to capital and technology could be channelled through an existing or new international body. It either case in should draw on the expertise of the World Bank, UNDP, UNCTAD, UNIDO and other competent international organisations to prevent that climate programmes hamper socio-economic development in the DCs.

The Climate Fund should not only address the greenhouse gases, especially CO_2, caused by the energy and deforestation sectors. It should also include, from the start, the phasing out of CFCs and, gradually, the reduction of the (other) greenhouse gases caused by agriculture, especially CH_4, and industry.

Finally, to cope with the damages of climate extremes which will become more frequent and intense with global warming, the Climate Fund should contain an 'emergency facility'. This should draw upon UNDRO and could be set up in the framework of the International Decade for Natural Disaster Reduction (1990s).

ICs would have to increase their investments by only ten per cent to ensure the co-operation of DCs, which would bear 75 per cent of their own investment costs. The Climate Fund would form an appropriate response to the UN General Assembly Resolution 43/53, recognising climate change as a 'common concern of mankind'.

REFERENCES

Blok, Kornelis *et al.*, 1989, 'The Role of Carbon Dioxide Removal in the Reduction of the Greenhouse Effect', University of Utrecht, Utrecht, 1989.
Brown, Lester R. *et al.*, 1987, *State of the World 1987* (and 1986), New York: W.W. Norton.
Beyond Oil, A Summary Report, 1986, Washington, DC: Carrying Capacity Inc. 1986.
Chandler, William U. *et al.*, 1988, 'Energy Efficiency: A New Agenda', American Council for An Energy-Efficient Economy, Washington, DC.
Ettinger, Jan van, 1989, *Energy and Environment in a Global Perspective.*
Gever, John *et al.*, 1986, *Beyond Oil, The Threat to Food and Fuel in the Coming Decades*, Cambridge, MA: Ballinger Publishing.
Goldenberg, Jose *et al.*, 1987, 'Energy for a Sustainable World', World Resources Institute, Washington, DC.
IEA/OECD, 1987a, *Energy Conservation in IEA Countries*, Paris: OECD.
IEA/OECD, 1987b, *Renewable Sources of Energy*, Paris: OECD.
IEA/OECD, 1989, *World Energy Statistics and Balances till 1987*, Paris: OECD.
International Conference on Global Warming and Climate Change: Perspectives from Developing Countries, New Delhi, February 1989, *Conference Statement.*
International Gas Union, Report of Committee J, 1988, *World Gas Supply and Demand, 1986–2020*, Paris.
International Panel on Climate Change, RSWG, 1989, *Draft Report of The US–Netherlands Expert Group on Emission Scenarios.*
International Workshop on A Little Breathing Space, 1989, Carbon Dioxide Emission Reduction Strategies, Budapest: Gerald Leach, *Africa.*
Keepin, Bill *et al.*, 1988, *Greenhouse Warming: Comparative Analysis of Two Abatement Strategies*, Energy Policy, Dec.
KNMI/RIVM, 1989, *Een paar graden meer?* (A Few Degrees More?; in Dutch), RIVM.
Kram, T. *et al.*, 1989, *Twee 'Laag CO_2' energiescenario's voor Nederland* (Two 'Low CO_2' Energy Scenarios for the Netherlands; in Dutch), in *Energiespectrum*, 89/3.
Leach, Gerald *et al.*, 1987, *Household Energy Handbook, an Interim Guide and Reference Manual*, TP 67, Washington, DC: World Bank.
Marchetti, Cesare, 1989, *Energy Generation Without CO_2 Emissions: Ecosystems Under Control?*, IIASA, Draft, Laxenburg.
Mintzer, Irving M, 1987, *A Matter of Degrees, The Potential for Controlling the Greenhouse Effect*, Washington, DC: World Resources Institute.
Odell, Peter R., 1988, *Long-Term Energy/Oil Forecasting Exercise 1988–2010*, EURICES, Rotterdam, (preliminary output).
Okken, P.A., 1987, *Energie en het broeikas effect* (Energy and the Greenhouse Effect; in Dutch), in *Energiespectrum* 40.
Sachs, Ignacy, 1989, 'Sustainable Development: From Normative Concept to Action', background paper seminar ISS/IDB, The Hague.
Soons, A.H.A., 1989, *Zeegrenzen en Zeespiegelrijzing* (Sea Borders and Sea Level Rise; in Dutch), Deventer: Kluwer.
Symposia on the Impact of Climate Change for the Third World, Washington, DC New York, March/June 1988: *Summary Report*, Climate Institute.
Trexler, Mark C. *et al.*, 1989, 'Forestry as a Response to Global Warming: An Analysis of the Guatamala Agroforestry and Carbon Sequestration Project', Draft, World Resources Institute, Washington, DC.
United Nations, 1982, *Energy Statistics Yearbook*, 1982 and later years, New York.
United States Environment Protection Agency, 1989, 'Policy Options for Stabilizing Global Climate', Draft Report to Congress, Washington DC.
Wiman, Bo L.B., 1989, 'On Global Environmental Futures: Some Problems, Attitudes and Policies', in Report No.3125, Lund University.
Wind, Herman G. (ed.), 1987, *Impact of Sea Level Rise on Society*, Rotterdam/Bookfield: A.A. Balkema.
World Bank, 1989, *World Development Report*, 1989 and earlier issues, Washington, DC.

World Bank/UNDP, 1988, *ESMAP Annual Report*, Washington, DC.

World Commission on Environment and Development, 1987, *Our Common Future*, Oxford/ New York: Oxford University Press.

World Conference on The Changing Atmosphere, 1988, 'Implications for Global Security', Toronto, June 1988: *Conference Statement*, Environment Canada.

World Congress on Climate and Development, Hamburg, Nov. 1988:

· Bach, Wilfrid, *Modeling the Climatic Effect of Trace Gases: Reduction Strategy and Options for a Low Risk Policy*;
· Burton, Ian, *To Limit and to Adjust: Some Human Dimensions of Global Climate Change*;
· Einhaus, Hans, *Preparations for the International Decade for Natural Disaster Reduction*;
· Nemec, J., *Climate and Development: Agriculture Practices and Water Resources*;
· Parry, Martin *et al.*, *Some Strategies of Response in Agriculture to Changes of Climate*;
· Potter, Thomas D., *Climate and Development – An Overview of International Developments, Trends and Actions*;
· Usher, Peter, *The International Response to Climate Change*.

World Resources Institute/International Institute for Environment and Development, 1988, *World Resources 1988–89*, New York: Basic Books.

World Resources Institute/National Climate Programme Office, 1988, 'Strategic Planning Seminar on the Long-Term Implications of Climatic Change'.

For Product Safety Concerns and Information please contact our EU
representative GPSR@taylorandfrancis.com
Taylor & Francis Verlag GmbH, Kaufingerstraße 24, 80331 München, Germany

www.ingramcontent.com/pod-product-compliance
Ingram Content Group UK Ltd.
Pitfield, Milton Keynes, MK11 3LW, UK
UKHW042200240425
457818UK00010B/313/J